The Successful Franchise Broker's Ultimate Networking Compendium

Frank Agin

Author of
Foundational Networking
Building Know, Like and Trust
To Create A Lifetime Of Extraordinary Succes

And Many Other Insightful Books On Achieving
Success Through Professional Networking

The Successful Franchise Broker's Ultimate Networking Compendium

Frank Agin

Printed in the United States of America

ISBN: 978-0-9823332-7-3

AmSpirit
BUSINESS CONNECTIONS

Post Office Box 30724
Columbus, Ohio 43230
Toll free: (888) 267-7474
Email: frankagin@amspirit.com

Ordering Information:
To order additional copies, contact 418 PRESS.
A Divison Of
Four Eighteen Enterprises LLC
Post Office Box 30724
Columbus, Ohio 43230-0724

Interior design: Hilary Jones
Cover Design: Kim Mettille of LogoTizeGraphicArtStudio.com

AmSpirit™
BUSINESS *CONNECTIONS*

Franchise Opportunity

The **AmSpirit Business Connections** franchise opportunity offers a great return on investment, as the initial fee is relatively low while at the same time the opportunity throws off significant cash with virtually no costs needed to operate it. For more detail on the **AmSpirit Business Connections** franchise opportunity, visit:

http://www.amspirit.com/franchise.php.

If you would like a complete overview of the program offered by **AmSpirit Business Connections**, contact Frank Agin and arrange a time to discuss how you or your client could benefit from this franchise opportunity.

Frank Agin, President
AmSpirit Business Connections
frankagin@amspirit.com

The Successful Franchise Broker's Ultimate Networking Compendium

Table Of Contents

AmSpirit™

BUSINESS *CONNECTIONS*

Franchise Opportunity

AmSpirit Business Connections is a service-based membership organization for entrepreneurs, sales representatives, and professionals. To become a member, these business types pay fees to belong and participate.

These members then meet each week (with an assigned group of other business types) for approximately one hour and 15 minutes to participate in a proprietary structured meeting format where they learn about one another's business and identify referral opportunities for each other.

Franchisees help these groups of members by helping them become larger and more productive in terms of referrals. Franchisees realize a return on their investment of time and money via the membership fees.

If you have a client that may be interested in a professional franchise opportunity or if you would like to learn more about **AmSpirit Business Connections**, contact Frank Agin at frankagin@amspirit.com.

Chapter 1

Here's To Your Success
Why Networking?

As a franchise broker, what is holding you back? What is preventing you from achieving success? Or what is preventing you from taking franchise brokering to the next level? What separates you from those brokers you hear about that experience dramatic results? What is keeping you from the results that you hoped for when you originally embarked onto franchise brokerage?

Could it be a better understanding of franchising? Perhaps you should know more about the Franchise Disclosure Document, almost being encyclopedic relative to Items 1 through 23. Maybe you need to know what is required in the various registration states, just in case someone asks. Or could it be that you need to have a better understanding as to how someone could fund their investment in a franchise opportunity? Might the level of franchising knowledge you have be holding you back from the success you aspire to?

Could it be that you have a lack of options? Right now, you are well versed in about 10 different franchise options. Maybe, if you expanded that offering to 20 or 30 that would lead to success. Perhaps it is not the number of options, but maybe the options are not diverse enough. Maybe you need to be well versed in a wide variety of franchise types and industry categories, literally something for everyone. Or perhaps, you need to narrow your focus, concentrating on a select few franchise types or industry categories. Might the amount of franchising options you are able to present too small (or big, or broad, or narrow)?

The simple answer to these questions are: No, No, and No. Certainly, a better technical understanding of any industry or business is a plus.

1

For your own credibility in working with clients, you should understand what Item 19 is all about, you should have a general idea as to what states are registration states, and you ought to have some clarity about franchising options. That said, your franchising knowledge is not holding you back from achieving the success you want.

Likewise, having the correct mix of franchise options is important to success. If it is too small, you likely won't have what a client wants. If, however, the portfolio of opportunities that you really understand is too large, you might not be able to adequately talk about any of them. Along the same lines, it would not be smart to focus on a particular franchise type or industry category (and neither would trying to understand them all). But still, your mix of franchise options is not holding you back from achieving the success you want.

So back to my original question, as a franchise broker, what is holding you back from achieving the success you aspire to? The answer, in a single word: CLIENTS. At this point, you likely know enough about franchising and you have enough franchise opportunity options at your finger tips to be successful. What you need are more clients.

If this describes you, do not despair. This issue is not limited to you. There are lacking dozens of franchise brokers reading this book coming to the same realization. In fact, this "lack of client" dilemma is not limited to franchise brokerage. Name a business or industry and you know that it is choked full of aspiring professionals with lots of technical knowledge and plenty to sell, but they have a dearth of clients.

This is the nature of business. Few people embark on business by saying, "I have a wonderful ability to build a client base, now let me learn about something to sell." It is usually just the opposite.

John the plumber has been toiling away for years at well-established ABC plumbing and has acquired all the necessary knowledge. John, however, has grown tired making someone else rich (conducting emergency calls on nights and weekends unclogging sinks and toilets). He wants to venture out on his own and does. He has all the technical ability in the world (the plumbing world), but he struggles to get clients.

Susan the real estate agent got into the profession because it fit perfectly with her lifestyle and family needs. She poured herself into all of her real estate classes. Susan seemingly knows everything about the profession. She even aced the licensing exam. With all that knowledge and proficiency, however, she struggles to find success. Why? She has no clients (and worse yet, she does not understand how to get them).

I even throw myself in this mix. After earning a law degree and finishing graduate business school, I got that highly prized position with a big name firm. After almost seven years, however, I was ready to take my accumulated knowledge and know-how into my own practice. It was the perfect plan. I was going to "WOW" the small business world with all that I knew. The problem was that no small businesses knew I was there. I had no idea how to get clients (and struggled until I figured out how to do it).

Again, do not despair. This is a struggle that most every business or profession encounters. And the world of franchise brokerage is no different. You (and most others) have all the knowledge and available products to be an incredible success. You likely struggle getting clients, much like lots and lots of franchise brokers do.

Many, many franchise brokers simply give up. Some of these failed brokers proclaim that the company that recruited them in (and educated them on) the business led them astray. Some will be upstanding and proclaim that they simply did not have the drive to make it work. Some just move on to something else (where client acquisition is not part of the formula for success).

Some franchise brokers, however, figure it out in time. That is, they have the knowledge and know-how plus they have been able to create a steady flow of clients. In getting there, they no doubt struggled through moments of trial and error. Some things they did were wonderfully successful. And some things they did, well, not so much. Worst of all, they did not understand why something worked and others didn't.

The purpose of this book is to lead you to success and short-circuit the trial and error. Here is the simple truth, in most any professional service type business the best, most reliable means of generating clients long term is via networking. In essence, professional networking creates a reasonably reliable pipeline of clients

The most successful real estate agents have a steady stable of clients and it is the result of their networking habits and practices. This is true of attorneys. It is true of mortgage lenders. It is the same for accountants, as well as insurance agents, financial advisors, and even plumbers. They each have networked themselves to create a steady pipeline of clients.

In fact, this is the case with pretty much any business or profession, which would include being a franchise broker. When things worked for a successful franchise broker, I am willing to bet that there was some element of sound professional networking. When things did not work, I am willing to bet that somehow professional networking was lacking (or not properly executed).

Who am I? I own and operate AmSpirit Business Connections, which focuses on assisting entrepreneurs, sales representatives, and professionals become more successful through networking. In short, we help our membership network with each other to find more customers and clients (and this program involves a wide variety of businesses and professions, including franchise brokers).

In addition, beyond AmSpirit Business Connections, I work with businesses and organizations of all sizes to understand business networking better as well as how to make the most effective use of it. To this end, I have written several books on professional networking and routinely talk on the topic of professional networking.

Everything in this book relates to and is connected with my work with the membership of AmSpirit Business Connections as well as my writings and teachings on professional networking. In short, this book will serve as a compilation of networking best practices, specifically geared towards becoming a successful franchise broker.

So if that is your aspiration – to become a successful franchise broker – you want a steady stream of clients. If that is the case, read on, take this book to heart, and put into practice everything I have included in it. This investment of your time will pay hefty dividends in the end.

Here's to your success!

AmSpirit

BUSINESS CONNECTIONS

Franchisee Profile

We are looking for entrepreneurs, sales representatives, or professionals with a reasonable track record of success, that have a strong need to become better networked, as well as have a desire and ability to help others grow and succeed via professional networking.

If you have a client that may be interested in plugging into this sort of professional franchise opportunity or if you would like to learn more about **AmSpirit Business Connections**, contact Frank Agin at frankagin@amspirit.com.

Chapter 2

Networking And
The Franchise Broker
What Does That Really Mean?

Introduction

Achieving success as a franchise broker is less about selling and more about developing relationships, often referred to as "networking." This chapter will give you an overview of the true essence of networking, explain the notion of social capital (the result of networking), and some basic ideas for networking success.

Networking Defined

Before we do anything more, let's settle on a working definition for networking.

Networking is two or more people working towards their mutual benefit. Simply put, networking is helping and being helped by others, and nothing more.

Given that definition, the universe of potential networking is very broad. The universe does include prospecting and selling, but it is much bigger than that. It also includes, servicing clients, attending events, volunteering, and, even socializing.

In fact, successful networking is something you need to focus on every waking moment. It is not something born out of the 80's, 90's or new millennium. It has been part of life since the beginning of the human existence. It has been part of everything in your life ... finding jobs and clients ... getting promotions ... finding a golf league, spouse, and babysitter (and not always in that order).

Three Reoccurring Themes

Networking is nothing new. In fact, it has been part of the discussion for years. As such, there are recurring themes within networking. If you come away from this book with nothing else, but understand these three concepts, you will be ahead of the vast majority of the working population.

1) The Golden Rule of Networking... This rule states that effective networking is about giving to others first (with no expectation of any return) and simply hoping that things will come back to you. Your entire networking existence should be about finding ways to help or give to others ... referrals, business, contacts, information, encouragement, your time ... give, give, give. Trust that, it will come back to you.

2) The Quintessential Elements Of Networking Relationships... All things being equal, we do business with people we know, like, and trust. In fact, all things being unequal, we still do things with those we know, like, and trust. So everything you do involving others needs to center on you getting to KNOW them (and not necessarily them you) ... you being perceived as LIKABLE to them ... and, you conducting yourself so they feel they can TRUST you.

3) Every Contact Has Opportunity ... We are all a little guilty of this: Dismissing some as not being of consequence to us. Know this, however, while everyone may not be your next franchising prospect, everyone is somehow connected to one (directly or indirectly). Thus, treat everyone as if they have that potential and eventually good things will follow.

The Appropriate Networking Mindset

Beyond understanding these three recurring networking themes, you also need to have the correct mindset, as attitude is everything:

Believe It Works ... Whether you believe networking will work or you don't, you are going to be right. If you believe in it, you will conduct yourself with confidence and that will draw people to you. If you are skeptical of the activity or its potential, that will serve to repel people from you. Thus, BELIEVE!

You Network Well ... Know this: Everything you do is networking. Everything you have ever achieved has involved networking. Everywhere you go you is networking. Everyone you interact with involves networking. Thus, you are much better at networking than you likely give yourself credit.

Be Of The Right Mind ... Not every day is going to be a good day. As such, if you are not in the right frame of mind (and cannot get there), save your networking for another day ... stay home ... off the phone ... away from e-mail.

Your Network Is An Asset

Your life is comprised of various assets. There is physical capital such as money, investments, homes, cars and other belongings. There is human capital, such as your ability to work, think and do things. And there is social capital, which the invisible benefit that a network can provide.

Know this, when you network, it is not an expense of your time. Do not think of it in those terms. Certainly some networking is more productive than others, but understand that any networking is an investment. Prospecting: An Investment. Attending An Event: An Investment. Volunteering: An Investment. Socializing: An Investment.

Think about networking as a component of building your personal wealth. When you network, you build value in your life.

Once you realize that your networking builds value in your life, the nature reaction is, "How much value do I have?" Certainly, this is not as simple as counting nickels and dimes or tallying hours worked. And while there are complicated formulas for assessing one's social capital, there are three rather simplistic means of gaining a thumbnail measurement of your social capital.

Connectivity. Answer this question "Who do I know?" Stop and think about it. Take an inventory of the people you know. High School. College. Neighbors. Community contacts. Church. The gym. And the list goes on and on. You likely know lots of people, and as you meet more your social capital grows.

Density. Think about it. If you knew ten people and those ten people all knew each other, your network is so dense (or interconnected) that the social capital is nowhere near as great as if you knew ten people and none of those people knew each other. So it is not just how many people you know that is important, but how many of those people know each other. Certainly, it is not reasonable to think that no one in your network knows anyone else, but you do want to have a broad, diverse network where you know lots of people and they are relatively disconnected from one another.

Potential. It is important how many people you know. And it is important how many of those people you know, know each other. But another means of assessing your network is to look through the people you know and see the people they know that you do not currently know. If you know ten people and they have relatively poor networks themselves, you are worse off than if you know only five people, but those five are extremely well connected.

Networking Opportunities ... A Broad Array

Your network brings value to you and there are ways of assessing the relative strength of your network. Now turn your attention to ways of networking. Networking opportunities fall into three distinct categories that we will touch on.

Face-To-Face Networking

These opportunities include various activities you would undertake when you are out and about with people.

Structured Networking, including Toastmasters, Rotary, Lions' Club, or organizations like AmSpirit Business Connections.

Networking Events, include trade shows, volunteer activities, business after-hours, Chamber events, seminars, and even social events like tailgates.

Free-Form Networking, includes perhaps a round of golf, meeting over a cup of coffee or, just getting together.

Electronic Encounters

With respect to networking in the modern age, much of what you can do face to face, you can accomplish via electronic means. More specifically, you network over the telephone, over e-mail, and through texting. Remember networking is more than selling and prospecting. *It is two or more people working towards their mutual benefit* – sharing referrals or contacts, passing on information, being encouraging and supportive.

Social Media

Finally, in the 21st century, technological innovation has given way to social media websites. These are nothing more than virtual venues where you can network – again, share referrals or contacts, pass on information, being encouraging and supportive.

The main three social media applications are LinkedIn, Facebook, and Twitter, but beyond these are dozens and dozens of others. Later in the book, I will do an entire chapter on using social media to network. Again, this is just a general overview of networking.

Nevertheless, know this about social media, if used properly, it will allow you to network on a massive scale, on a worldwide basis, 24 hours a day and seven days a week, and do so with incredible information about your networking partner before you even make contact.

Overview ... What Does That Really Mean?

There is tremendous value in networking and networking adds value to you. Networking is much more than prospecting and selling. In general, it involves interacting with those around you (face-to-face, over the telephone, e-mail or text, and even using social media). Nevertheless, you engage in networking for the purpose of helping the people around you and at the same time position yourself to receive help.

To conclude know this, Networking Works.

Now it may not work HOW you would like it to work. For example, you go to a networking event hoping to meet accountants who might know of people interested in buying a franchise. To that end, nothing pans out, but you do learn of a job-transition group that you were not aware of. Networking did not work HOW you wanted, but it worked.

Networking may not work WHERE you want it to work. The next day standing in line to get coffee, you strike up a conversation with someone who reveals in polite conversation that they are looking for more freedom in their professional life. Networking did not work WHERE you wanted, but it worked.

Finally, networking may not work WHEN you want it to work. For example, again, you go to a networking event hoping to make contacts to help you find clients interested in franchising. You seem to come up empty. Then a month later, a year later, or even a decade (or more) later, someone reconnects with you from that event looking to be your client. Trust me, this happens. Again, Networking did not work WHEN you wanted, but it worked.

AmSpirit™

BUSINESS CONNECTIONS

Can I Get You A Tie?

The savvy tailor does not shy away from selling ties. Certainly, the big money is in selling that custom-made suit. Whether or not the parton purchases a suit, however, the savvy tailor will sell them a tie - earning a tidy little profit on a simple, but colorful, piece of silk.

Figuratively speaking, you are a tailor and all the franchise opportunities you have are like suits, almost custom fitted to each individual client. While the price of these suits range, they are the source of your big money.

Following this metaphor, the **AmSpirit Business Connections** franchise opportunity is like the tie. It may not represent big money to you, but it can be a tidy little profit, if you let it.

When you stumble across the person who could not possibly afford a suit, consider **AmSpirit Business Connections.** This opportunity has a low initial required investment - a little more than $10,000.

The **AmSpirit Business Connections** franchise opportunity may not be big monet, but it does represent a tidy little profit. So, be like the savvy tailor and don't shy away from selling a tie or two.

For more information on the **AmSpirit Business Connections**, contact Frank Agin at frankagin@amspirit.com.

Chapter 3

Effectively Networking The Franchise Broker
Psst... It's More Than Who You Know

Introduction

Being a franchise broker requires knowledge about all facets of franchising. Being successful, however, is less about what you know about franchising and more about whom you know. This is generally a function of networking. In this chapter, I am going to give practical advice on making the best out of those people you know.

Sage Advice Or Partial Myth

No doubt, at one point you heard the statement: "It's Not What You Know, But Who You Know." Chances are, that is something you have heard once or twice in your life, from a well-meaning parent, a mentor, or supportive colleague. This begs the question, "How much truth is there to this?"

In reality, this is sage advice, but at the same time, it is also partially a myth. Why is this? Who you know is more important than what you know. The world has more than its share of brilliant people that fall far, far from their true potential because they study away on incredible scholarly projects all by themselves.

At the same time, far less brilliant people rise to great heights merely on the connections they have. For example, Bill Gates was not the smartest computer person going. He was simply a smart computer mind with a plethora of connections.

But as much as who you know is important, the world also has more than its share of individuals that seemingly know lots of people but get very little from this network. How is this possible? Quite simply, it is more than who you know.

It Is The Relationship

Effective networking is not just about knowing people. And it is so much more than making dozens of calls, posting on social media, and attending events. This is the simple reality: effective networking is not just about connecting with and be connected to others. Effective networking is about having meaningful relationships with those you are connected with.

As a franchise broker, success will not come from filling your database with dozens, hundreds, or even thousands of people. You will achieve success by creating relationships with a reasonable number of people.

These can include centers of influences (such as, bankers, attorneys, accountants, outplacement professionals).

These relationships could also be with existing franchisees, which have a network of family, friends, and acquaintances that want a similar professional existence.

These relationships could be with a wide variety of different types of people directly, indirectly, and even seemingly completely unrelated to franchising.

Whatever the case, the important thing is that you have a solid RELATIONSHIP with them.

Know, Like & Trust

So, effective networking is predicated on building solid relationships. That almost begs the question, "How do I create solid relationships?"

We serve to create solid relationships with people in our lives when we set about to make three things happen, and these can be distilled down into three simple words: Know, Like & Trust.

You build relationships when you get people to know you and you get to know others;

You build relationships when you get the people you set about getting to know to like you; and

You build relationships when you do the things that allow other people to trust you.

Here is a simple reality; People do business with people they know, like and trust. You do business with people you know, like and trust. All things being equal, you will do business with someone you know, like and trust.

All things being equal, you likely have the accountant, banker, or financial planner in your life because you know, like and trust them. In fact, all things being unequal, you would still opt to do business with the person you know, like and trust. Think about it. If you have automobile insurance, there is no question you could find the same coverage for less. Yet, you stay with the same agent. Why? You know, like and trust the person.

This is a powerful component of human nature. If you can get people coming to that conclusion that they know, like and trust you (this is at a very gut level), they will more likely be moved to help you ... refer you candidates ... introduce you to centers of influence

... direct you towards beneficial opportunities.

The $ 64,000 Question

Understanding that"know, like and trust" is extremely powerful, begs another question: "How can I go about getting others to know, like and trust me?"

In the world of business and professional networking, that is the $64,000 question. The balance of this chapter reviews seven actions or insights that serve to build know, like and trust.

1) Never Stop Giving

The Golden Rule of Networking is "give first, get second." In short, if you want to get things from your network, you need to give to it. Focus on giving to others … give referrals … give additional contacts … give opportunities … give information … give encouragement … give support … give, give, give.

When you give to others they cannot help but know, like and trust you. As a result, the people you give to will want to return the generosity. In addition, you will develop the reputation of being a "generous person." This will inspire others to want to contribute to you, as they come to believe that you are likely to give back.

This is a powerful strategy and should become almost a daily habit.

Share information with your fellow franchise brokers and they will share information back.

Give referrals to centers of influence in your network and they will go out of their way to return the deed.

Help your prospective clients with things unrelated to buying a franchise and you will be forever on the top of their mind (perhaps referring you clients down the road).

Be supportive of those you have helped purchase a franchise and they will "rave" to others about you.

With everyone you encounter, ask yourself, "In what way could I help them?" When the answers come to you, take action. That will build know, like, and trust like nothing else.

2) Every Contact Has Opportunity

It is easy to do and we are all guilty of it – dismissing someone as being of little or no consequence to us. Maybe it was a gas station attendant. Maybe it was a receptionist. Maybe it was the kid delivering the paper.

Know this, however, while everyone may not be your next prospective client, everyone knows someone that might be. Not everyone will fit neatly into your network as a center of influence, but everyone is connected to someone who could. Not everyone is going to be chalked full of useful information, but you can bet they sure know a person who is.

In short, everyone has value and every relationship has potential. Knowing this, everyone deserves and should receive the respect and attention that you would offer your best clients, your key centers of influence, or your prime information sources. If you consistently do this, everyone will know, like and trust you (and people who do not know you will want to somehow be associated with you).

3) There Is No Shame In Asking

Call it "human nature" or call it the "American Spirit," but we are hardwired to help one another.

Certainly the aftermath of the events of September 11th (or any major tragedy) make this abundantly clear. People will go to great lengths to help one another.

With this, the only thing that separates you from the help that you need is you asking. Dare to ask. Remember, if you are focused on giving and helping others, it is only fair that you attempt to partake from the same process.

- Let others know what kind of help you want.

- Describe the types of people you are trying to meet.

- Explain to your centers of influence how they can help you.

- Solicit people for information on job transition groups or opportunities to present on the benefits of franchising.

Understand this, if you are polite in asking of others and appreciative of whatever they give (even if it is only time), people will come through. Not everyone, but enough to make it all worthwhile.

Equally important, however, when you reach out to others, you are in essence affirming that they have value to offer. It is a wonderful compliment. For that, they will be flattered. As backwards as it might seem, they will know, like, and trust you for reaching out to them.

4) Work To Get Involved

To be a successful franchise broker, you cannot just hole-up in front of your computer and work the phone. You need to shower up, brush your teeth, and get out amongst people. Find groups and organizations to join.

Know this, however, you cannot just belong. You cannot just be in the community. You cannot just be in the Chamber. You cannot just be part of the Church. You cannot just belong.

To effectively network. To develop strong relationships by building know, like, and trust,-you have to get involved. Roll up your sleeves (actually or figuratively) and lend a hand. Be an officer in a group. Be a committee member of an organization. Be something (anything) more than just a name on a membership roster.

Here is the test as to whether you are sufficiently involved, answer this: If you didn't show up, would you be missed? If the answer is no, you need to work harder to get involved. By doing so, you raise your level of exposure and demonstrate your level of commitment to something more than just you. When you do these things, others will not be able to help but know, like, and trust you.

5) One Relationship At A Time

Your network (or any network, for that matter) is built one relationship at a time. There is an Indian proverb that says, "An eagle that chases two rabbits, catches none." This is true of relationships as well.

You will not be able to develop lasting know, like and trust if you are focused on multiple relationships at any one time. In fact, the more relationships you attempt to develop at once, the less effective you become.

The point to this topic is this: As you are out being involved, do not feel the need to race about meeting as many people as possible, having quick, shallow conversations, collecting business cards and then haphazardly following up with a plethora of people you can hardly remember.

Rather work to have involved conversations with just a few

people (and then attend another gathering and do the same). Learn about people. Invest time in who they are. Be genuinely interested. Conduct yourself so that when you follow up, you can do so with substance.

By working to develop relationships one person at a time, you become more effective developing relationships, in short people will know, like and trust you.

6) Remember To Reconnect

Whether you are 19, 90 or somewhere in between, you now know more people than you could possibly meet over the next year (maybe two or three). Think about it. You know people in your community. You know people from high school, college, and your plethora of career moves (or those moving careers around you). You know people through your kids, parents, or family. You know lots of people.

While meeting new people is always an important part of networking, there is a tremendous advantage to networking with familiar names and faces – they already know, like and trust you. That is a tremendous head start to productive and effective networking.

Given that, an important part of building your franchise brokerage network, is to dig into your "now electronic" rolodexes, card files or little black books and mine your existing contacts. Reconnect with these old friends and acquaintances. Get caught up on their lives. Think of ways you can help them. Share with them about your professional endeavor in franchising and remember to "dare to ask." Something as simple as, "If you ever know of someone interested in exploring franchising, please forward them on to me."

Remember the "know, like, and trust" is already there. All you need to do is capitalize on it.

7) Keep After It

As a franchise professional, you need clients today. Guess what? You are going to need them tomorrow, and the next day, and next year. Thus, creating and nurturing productive relationships is an ongoing endeavor. Your job is never done.

Know this: Some days your networking efforts are going to seem worthwhile. It is easy to keep after it. Other days your networking efforts are going to seem like a complete waste. You will want to swear it off. Don't.

You need to have faith. Opportunity comes from the most unlikely places and it is all the result of productive relationships. Never quit trying to build Know, Like, and Trust.

More Than Who You Know

To summarize, remember to be a successful franchise broker, knowing about franchising is important. What is vital, however, is being proficient at networking. Networking, though, is about building solid relationships where people know you, like you, and trust you. Those things are achieved through certain actions and interactions with those in your network. These actions involve consistent generosity, reliability, and commitment to others, just to mention a few.

AmSpirit

BUSINESS *CONNECTIONS*

An Opportunity With A Great ROI

AmSpirit Business Connections is a great program to empower small business people to greater success and it is a wonderful franchise opportunity as it offers a great return on investment via:

- A Very Low Initial Required Investment

- An Attractive Ongoing Revenue Stream

- Extremely Low Operating Expenses

If you have a client that is interested in learning more about the great return on investment offered by the **AmSpirit Business Connections** franchise opportunity, contact Frank Agin at frankagin@amspirit.com.

Chapter 4

Successful Events
For The Franchise Broker
Effectively Working The Room

Introduction

Achieving success as a franchise broker is about effective networking. That said, networking events are a great place, to well, network. Despite this, some franchise brokers have been known to avoid them because they are unsure as to how they should conduct themselves. In this chapter, I will empower you with the insights and confidence to feel at home in any setting.

Avoiding Events

According to research, among the fears of a great many people are 1) Death by fire; 2) Public speaking; and 3) Vacationing with in laws

Shortly behind those is finding ones self in a room of total strangers. And, even if you don't fear that situation, you might not be totally comfortable with it. But it does not have to be this way.

Whenever the topic of networking is discussed, the notion of how to connect with strangers always seems to come up and it is always accompanied with a degree of anxiety.

Ten Step Plan

There are, however 10 simple steps that any franchise broker can employ to ensure that they have a great experience at any event.

1. Frame Of Mind

The first step is to ensure that you **Have The Right Frame of Mind**. While this might not need mentioning, there are plenty of people who trip themselves up at networking events before they actually show up.

First, remember that networking works. At any particular event it might not work exactly how you want it, but before you embark on the networking event, you need to truly believe that the networking process works and your mere presence has set that in motion.

While your mere presence is important, you will totally undermine your efforts if you bring with you anything but a positive disposition. No, not every day (month or year, for that matter) can be a good one, however, there is something good about each. Reflect on the positive aspects of your personal and professional life. Do what you can to be of uplifting spirits. Remember, while support groups can be a networking opportunity, most networking events are not designed to be support groups. Leave your worries at the door, to the extent possible.

Finally, embark on any networking event with a sincere expectation something will come from it. Now, it might not be all that you hoped for. After all, there is no guarantee (or even likelihood) that you will get a client out of it. Know this, however, something will come from you being there.

You might meet someone that can refer you clients. You might meet someone that puts you one step closer to that. You might reconnect with a former client or center of influence. You might gain a piece of information that holds all sorts of value. There is a plethora of potential benefit that can come from any networking event. You will never get it all, but you will always likely get something.

2. Opportunities From Anybody

As a second step remember from last chapter that **Every Contact Has Opportunity**. Again, we are all guilty of this: dismissing someone as having no positive consequence to our lives. No, not everyone is going to be your next best client, your next great referral partner, or quality vendor. What is true, however, is that everyone (absolutely everyone) is somehow connected to someone who could be.

Business opportunities come from all sorts of different sources and business opportunities will find their way to you from all sorts of different directions. You know that. You likely also know that you cannot predict where that next client is coming from or from what direction.

Given that, you simply cannot make judgments about the value of people reactive to your business objectives. After all, someone you think will be a great source for you, might offer nothing. Conversely, someone you never expected to offer any value to you provides you the Mother Lode. You just never know.

Thus, do not dismiss someone (or anyone) of being of no consequence to you. This is not to suggest that everyone needs to be within your contact database or that you need to invite everyone to your open house party. It does suggest that you treat everyone with the same respect and attention as you would approach someone that you knew had a great business opportunity for you.

3. Location, Location, Location

At the event Appropriately Position yourself. In fishing, you go to where the fish are or will be. In networking, the same logic holds. Stand where you will most likely be amongst people. Near the entrance. At the buffet or bar. Close to other high traffic areas.

If you stand outside the main stream of human flow (or worse, sit off to the side), you virtually eliminate your opportunity for having anything come from the networking event – immediately or ever.

4. Make Contact

Assuming you have positioned yourself appropriately, you will encounter people. Like a parade, from your position people will go meandering by.

In step four it is simply up to you to **Initiate Contact**. That is worth repeating, it is up to you to initiate contact. Alternatively stated, DO NOT wait (or expect) others to make contact with you. Making contact is 100% your obligation, if you want a productive experience.

There is no magic to initiating contact. It only involves three simple things.

1) Make meaningful eye contact with people, where you look at them in the eye and they look you back at you. There is nothing strange about this. It is completely human.

2) With eye contact established, smile. This is not a forced smile, but a genuine "it is good to see you" smile. Chances are, human nature will kick in and they will smile back.

3) With that eye contact and a smile, simply say, "hello." They may say "hello" in return, or they may say nothing.

Whatever the case, it was your objection (as well as sole obligation) to initiate contact. You have done that. Congratulations.

This sounds simple and it is. Nevertheless, this may be a little out of your comfort zone. If it is, here is a great way to practice. Go anywhere there are people (for example, shopping) and simply wander around naturally making eye contact, smiling, and saying, "hello." It may seem unnatural at first, but in time you will develop a level of comfort that you can utilize in a more professional setting.

5. Converting Contacts To Connections

At this moment – after making eye contact, smiling, and saying hello – one of two things will happen.

1) Nothing will happen, as they will just move along. So what? Don't take it personal. There could be a dozen or more reasons why they did not stop and none of them related to you.

2) They stop and are open to expanding the mere contact into a more meaningful connection, which leads you into step five.

When this happens, ensure to do these three things...

1) Handshake ... First, offer your hand in anticipation of a handshake, the true first impression. The handshake should be firm, intersecting your thumb web with theirs. Do not make your handshake too hard – a bone crushing that might serve to imply dominance. Moreover, do not make your handshake too soft – a limp fish that might serve to imply disinterest. Make that handshake firm, but nothing spectacular. Remember, you are best to not be remembered for your handshake as opposed to being remembered for a bad one.

2) Offer Your Name ... Second, as you shake hands, offer your name. In so doing, be sure to enunciate you first name clearly. In addition, to further the connection, there are two other reasons as to why this is important. First, unless they are someone you know well, by offering your name you serve to eliminate any potential embarrassment to them for not remembering your name from an earlier encounter. Second, when you offer your name, they are likely to offer theirs in return.

3) Clarify Their Name ... When you offer your name, if they do not recite theirs, ask them, "What is your name?" Whatever the case, when they offer their name (whether they did it initially or you had to prompt them), clarify their name aloud. For example,

"Hello, my name is Susan."

"Great to meet you, Susan. Correct?"

You might also consider clarifying what they prefer to be called (e.g., Do you go by Susan, Sue, or either or?"). These steps will help you better remember their name. In addition, it will subtly imply that their name is important to you.

6. Make Small Talk

Once you have exchanged names, conversation will likely ensue. Step six suggests you **Engage In It**. While the next chapter is on carrying this conversation, here are some high points.

Do not start the conversation directly focused on business or professional aspects. That can be off-putting and serve to create an uncomfortable situation. Rather, engage in some small talk. Inquire as to the origin of their name. Ask them about their impressions on the event itself. Get them talking on anything other than business. This will serve to make the connection comfortable.

After a few minutes (or even several minutes of small talk), segue over to more professional topics. Ask about their business. How long have they done it? What did they do before? How did they get started?

Once the professional discussion has run its course, segue back to small talk. You can reflect on something professional they said, and tie it back to something within small talk.

7. Listen Intently

Under step seven, as you engage in conversation, be sure to listen to what they have to say. **Focus On Them**, and not your watch, or who is coming through the door, or anything going on around you.

You should express a genuine interest in what they have to say, especially if it is a topic that you set in motion with one of your questions. To do this, face up to them, make eye contact, and:

Make sounds and comments to indicate understanding (or a simply nod your head) ... "Oh, interesting."

Ask questions to clarify things ... "Now, when you [blank], do you mean?

Echo back what they have said in summary fashion ... "So you basically got into business because ..."

As they talk Look For Things You Have In Common, whether they are shared backgrounds, similar experiences, or ways to relate to them. You can use these to interject or ask questions, as a means of keeping the conversation going.

8. Find A Way To Help

No doubt you are networking to get things ... clients, important contacts, and other information. Understand this: They are two. This is the eighth step, you can make an indelible impression on them by finding some way of Helping Them – even if only in a small way. So as they talk, run whatever they are saying through a filter that queries: "How can I add value to them?" This is the Golden Rule of Networking – Give First And Get Second.

There is nothing that says that you have to help them right there and now. If you can help them in that moment, great. If not, do not despair. Just understand that you make the most of building that connection by trying to find some way you can add value. It might be a referral. It might be a contact. It might be important information for them.

9. Gracefully Move On

As wonderful as that connection is, do not burn out the conversation. **Move On To Other People**. This is not to say that you need to use the event to get out handfuls of your business cards and collect handfuls in return. That is not productive either.

The ninth step means that you should attempt to connect enough with the person so that you are both comfortable continuing the conversation another time. Perhaps that is at the next event. Perhaps that is over coffee the next week. Whatever the case, get their contact information and pledge to get back to them.

This will allow you the opportunity to meet and connect with other people. To this end, when you find a lull in the conversation, simply suggest to them:

"I would love to keep talking, but ...

"I don't want to occupy your whole time …"

"There are a couple people I need to connect with before the event is over;" or,

"I promised myself that I would meet three new, great contacts today ... you make one and now I need to find two others."

"If you do not mind, however, I would like to reach out to you later this week (early next week) and arrange a time where we can continue this conversation."

10. Follow Up, As Promised

The tenth and final step is to Follow Up or Follow Through regarding whatever you promised to. If you pledged to reconnect, do so. If you offered to introduce them to someone else, make it happen. If you indicated you would send them something, get it sent.

Know this, so few people follow through on what they say they are going to do. That is a sad, but true fact. Given that, if you are committed to doing so, you immediately elevate yourself ahead of a significant portion of the population.

Three Final Thoughts

People often ask, how can you determine whether a networking event is worthwhile or not. There is no answer for that. They all have value. Some offer more immediate value than others. The best advice is to simply attend events following the 10 steps a discussed herein, and trust that in time opportunities will find their way to you.

Nevertheless, there are three final thoughts on making the most of networking events.

First, networking events are generally not opportunities for closing business. Thus, you will not likely get clients as a result of them. You may stumble upon a client. Know, however, that is the a exception rather than the rule.

Second, as you embark upon networking at events, do not consume

yourself with meeting as many people as you can. a
Remember, meaningfully connecting is about the quality of the connection and not the quantity. You are much further ahead in time to focus on really connecting with a small handful of people rather than simply collecting dozens of business cards.

Third, remember, networking events are everywhere. Business after-hours are networking events. Tradeshows are networking events. Business parties are networking events as well as social parties, tailgates, and really any gathering of people. With that, starting with today, use each gathering of people as a wonderful setting to set the networking process in motion.

Chapter 5

Conversations With The Franchise Broker
Big Things From Small Talk

Introduction

Achieving success as a franchise broker is less about selling and more about developing relationships. Often developing a relationship is as simple as having a casual conversation with prospective candidates.

Unfortunately, this "small talk" tends to get a bad rap of being useless and time wasting. This chapter will not only explain how and why "small talk" leads to wonderful networking relationships, but also give insights on how to make good small talk and use it to your advantage.

Small Talk Has A Bad Reputation

Let's face it: "small talk" has a bad reputation. It probably dates back to the continual chiding our Mother's did relative to talking with strangers.

While her warnings were intended to protect us as children from those who prey on our innocence, we are no longer kids. We are big boys and girls. We operate in the grown-up world where strangers become good friends, great clients and, even, reliable vendors.

Even still, however, "small talk" gets a bad rap. Far too often people see it as idle chitchat that has no productive value in the professional world. Understand this, our entire personal and professional worlds are formed and held firmly together by networking. And "small talk" has a big part in successful networking.

Networking Defined (Again)

As I stated earlier: Networking Works. It may not work exactly *how* you want. It may not work exactly *when* you want. It may not work exactly *where* you want. But it works.

Essentially, again, in networking you are creating a series of relationships. The end game is that you want the network to help you. Thus, in order to build the strong network of contacts that are both willing and able to refer you clients, three things need to happen. They need to KNOW you. They need to LIKE you. And, they need to TRUST you.

Remember: All things being equal, people do business with those they know, like and trust. In fact, all things being unequal, people tend to do business with those they know, like and trust. (Like the same insurance agent for years, even though you know you could get less expensive insurance elsewhere.)

Small Talk's Role

How does this all relate to "small talk"? Think about it. What did you do that last time you were at an event and someone launch into business immediately.

"Who does your printing? Are you happy? I can do better? Give me a chance. Throw me some business? Well, why not?"

It is through "small talk" that people gain an understanding of: Who you are ... What interests you ... How you spend your time. And you learn the same about them.

As an analogy, "small talk" is like the warm up you do before you really get into the work out. It is the foundation of the

KNOWING in know, like and trust. It is also this small foundation, upon which people gain a sense as to whether they LIKE you. In fact, social science and brain studies have shown that in the few minutes where chitchat is happening, people even start to formulate a sense as to whether or not they TRUST you too.

Apprehension Rears Its Head

This all makes sense. And yet there is an apprehension towards "small talk". For many, it comes down to one thing FEAR. Fear of being rejected. Fear of having nothing to contribute. Fear of getting stumped (or running out of conversation). Fear of getting stuck in a conversation with, well, that stranger that Mom warned you about.

FEAR NOT! The strangers your mother warned you about are no longer interested. You have things to contribute and with a little planning and practice you will never get stumped (and if you do, there is a way out).

As for rejection, know this: Everyone has this fear. EVERYONE. Even the most well connected, confident person will tell you that deep down inside, that they have this apprehension. If everyone has this fear, then everyone will welcome you coming up and jumping into conversation with them.

The Simple Game Plan

Here is the most important thing to understand: "Small talk" is not about filling idle time with interesting things to say. Rather, "small talk" is about getting the other person filling idle with things to say and you genuinely finding interest in it.

To make this happen, like anything, the key to success in "small talk" is having a reliable game plan. Like most game plans, the simplest ones are the best ones and this is the simplest, most reliable game plan I have seen going.

Step One: Ask A Question

Now remember, the key is to get them talking, so you need to be ready with questions that are open-ended. **"Isn't this weather crazy?,"** will not cut it. **"How does this crazy affect you?,"** just might. Let's return to the notion of good questions to ask in a minute.

Step Two: Listen ... Really Listen

Take an interest in what they have to say, even if the subject is not particularly interesting to you. Why? First, you just might learn something (something that could help you, or something that you can use to help them (which ultimately helps you)).

Second, and this is very counterintuitive, but if you take an interest in them and whatever they have to say, they will find you to be a very interesting person (and they will not know why). It is just human nature. People tend to like people who show a genuine interest in them. So this listening encourages the entire networking process.

Step Three: Summarize & Share

As a follow-up (to show you are really listening), summarize what you have heard (or at least do the best you can) and then share a little about the subject as it relates to you. *"So, as an avid water skier all this hot weather is great. I find that it kills my golf game."*

Then finally (just like the instruction on the shampoo bottle - lather, rinse and repeat), ask another question. Perhaps it is related to the first question, or maybe it is another tangent you would like to explore based on what they said in their answer. For example, *"So, if hot weather is good, what do you do to occupy yourself when it is too cold to take to the lake?"*

The $64,000 Question

Now the $64,000 question is "What are the best questions to ask?" The answer to this depends; depends on who you are asking questions of.

There is no magic. Planning, however, is paramount. Be like an attorney – prepare your questions before you ask them. In other words, have a small handful of questions ready to go. Each of these relate to the person's life professionally or personally, or something about their past. From there, simply allow the conversation to take itself wherever.

Here are some questions you can consider adding to your arsenal:

What do you do? How long have you been doing it? How did you become interested in that?

What are some of the projects or assignments you are currently working on?

Are you from this area?

Yes – What part?

No – What brought you here?

Outside of work, what occupies you? How did you become interested in that?

What are some business or community organizations you are involved with?

Or you might want to formulate your own series of questions. Again, there is no magic. It is simply a matter of planning on how you will get and keep them talking.

Leveraging Small Talk

Now remember, "small talk" is just the warm-up and thus it should lead to a work out. The work out is talking business.

Transition To Business

When this moment comes, you will know. Some time into your exchange, there will be a lull. Use this moment to get at a more meaty discussion on business (whatever that might be). Be forewarned, however, this is not to suggest that you start to pitch them or set them up for a close. It merely suggests that once you have them comfortably engaged in conversation, you can ease into a more professional discussion of their business or your business.

Returning to our example, here might be a good segue ... *"Well, water skiing is likely not cheap ... So what do you do professionally to pay for it?"*

Do not try to steer them. For example a business coach, should not ask ... *"Do you use business coaches in your business?"* ... A financial advisor, should not go with ... *"How is your 401K doing these days?"* ... A promotional products person, should not jump to ... *"How do you use ad specialty items in your business?"*

Do NOT push it. Keep the tone light and the probing to a minimum. If you do this right, you will have lots of opportunity to gather future business intelligence, pitch them, and close them. Remember, know, like and trust.

Return To Small Talk

After the professional conversation has run its course, before the conversation ends, touch back on something related to your "small talk" conversation. Returning to the example, *"Great talking with you. Assuming, you don't get laid up in the hospital skiing between now and then, I would enjoy continuing our con-*

versation over a cup of coffee sometime."

Why is this important? By returning to "small talk", you have demonstrated that you were listening and that you remembered. More subtly, however, you are reflecting back to a part of the conversation when they likely delighted in your interest in them.

Exit Gracefully

Whatever the case, do not churn the entire event away in a single conversation. Nothing says that you need to engage in a dozen different conversations over the course of an hour. Two or three is plenty.

Remember this is not speed dating. Given that, you should develop some ways of moving on. As with anything else, honesty is the best policy. The last chapter provided some, but here are some more lines for gracefully moving on:

"There is someone over there that I need to connect with."

"Is there anyone here in particular you would like to meet? I would be glad to introduce you."

Improving Small Talk

"Small talk" is not an art. You can certainly, however, improve how you do it through practice. Here are some ideas for becoming more proficient at it.

Think ... On the way to the next event or when you have some idle time, work through in your mind how you envision your "small talk" going. Review your questions in your mind. See yourself listening, summarizing, and sharing.

Listen ... "Small talk" is all around you, everyday. Listen to it, especially to those who are good at it. See how they weave from one question to the next and how they transition to business, return to small talk and then exit the conversation.

Engage ... Take every opportunity to engage in "small talk." When you are in line at the store check out. With a server in a restaurant. With the receptionist at your next appointment. You will find the more you engage in small talk, the more comfortable you get at it.

"Small Talk" Self-Talk

The most important thing you need to have in being good at "small talk" is an attitude or belief.

Periodically, you need to tell yourself (especially when those voices of doubt start to speak up in your head) *"I can carry a conversation. I can. I am good at it. I enjoy it. I like how it lifts the spirits of others. And I love what it is doing for my networking. I can carry a conversation."*

If you plan out a good series of questions, continually remind yourself that you are good at "small talk", and then practice "small talk" in non-threatening situations, you will NOT only become great at it, but you will really start to enjoy it. Best of all, you will derive lots of great benefits from it.

Chapter 6

Pitching The Franchise Broker
An Effective 30-Second Message

Introduction

Well-established, successful franchise brokers will tell you that it is important to build a strong network of contacts (friends, relatives, and strategic partners) that are willing and able to refer you clients. To create this, this strong network of contacts need to *know* you, *like* you and *trust* you.

In establishing this "know, like and trust," these people need to have a firm sense as to ... *Who* you are ... *What* you do ... *Why* they should refer you... and, *How* they can help you.

The primary limitation to conveying this information (especially amongst people you have met for the first time) is simply attention span. In somewhere around 30 seconds, you need to effectively communicate all these things, or risk losing their minds to something (or someone) else. In short, you need to have a concise, yet compelling, 30-second commercial.

In this chapter is a framework (along with examples) that serves as a guide for building a great 30-second commercial.

Framework & Idea Examples

An effective 30-second commercial has four basic parts ... the Who (*Basic Introduction*) ... the What (*Message Body*) ... the Why (*Inspire Confidence*) ... and, the How (*Strong Definite Request*).

To build a great commercial, draft a short statement for each of the sections below. With these, piece them together to create a succinct and convincing case for Y-O-U.

Basic Introduction

Start your 30-second commercial with a quick overview of yourself and your business.

There is nothing fancy about this, but it is important to convey *who you are*, however. Some examples of this basic introduction could include:

I am John Doe, a franchise broker with National Franchising Group.

I am John Doe with National Franchising Group -- essentially, I am a franchise broker.

I am a franchise broker with National Franchising Group. My name is John Doe.

Message Body

The next component is the heart or main section of your 30-second commercial. In it, you are indicating *what you do*.

While the basic introduction is generally plain vanilla, in this message body you can inject some creativity. You could be informative. On the other hand, you might consider being somewhat amusing. Or, if appropriate, you might consider grabbing their attention with something unexpected or startling.

Here are some relevant examples of effective message bodies:

Through the program and processes at National Franchising Group, I help individuals identify, analyze and secure the best franchise for them based on their financial situation, desired lifestyle and professional interests.

Over 80% of all businesses fail within the first five years of opening. The ones that survive are generally franchised operations. I work with my clients to find the right franchised business for them so that they can be amongst the successful.

I coach people on how to tell their bosses to "take this job and shove it." I work with everyday individuals and help them realize the dream of business ownership by connecting them with one of the 1,000's of franchised businesses available.

Inspire Confidence

At this point, you have artfully established the "who" and the "what" for yourself. If you stop there, however, that will only beg the question, *"Why you?"*

There are literally hundreds and hundreds of franchise brokers, and more entering the profession every day. What makes you unique amongst them?

On top of that, there are all the attorneys, accountants and financial planners with little-to-no training, but the firm belief (right or wrong) that they can help their clients find the right franchise as well as you.

Neither of these is your biggest competition, however. Your biggest competition is person with $500,000 in his pocket who believes he (or she) can do it on his (or her) own.

Again, "why you?" Your commercial needs to convey credibility and confidence that serves to answer that question before your prospective client (or center of influence) even asks it. Let's consider an example.

Not only have I helped more than 100 people get into the right franchise, I also spent 10 years as a CPA.

National Franchising Group has over 300 professionals around the country and has helped thousands of people over the last 20+ year.

Along with our nationwide team of brokers, we have developed a unique process for getting people the right franchise.

Strong Definite Request

Now you have clearly articulated *who you are*, appropriately stated *what you do* and effectively indicated *why you* are uniquely qualified to serve a prospective client. At this point, however, in a sense, it is like having a "souped up" car with no wheels.

To complete your 30-second commercial, you need to state clearly *how you need* assistance. Most 30-second commercials have a weak finish. This is mainly because they have a feeble ask or request.

An example of a feeble request would be:

"A good referral for me is someone in transition or not happy with the direction of their career."

This is merely a statement. It completely lacks a request for someone to do something. To avoid this pitfall and set yourself apart, your 30-second commercial should have a "call to action," or definitive request for the person to do something. Some examples of this are:

If you know of someone in transition or not happy with the direction of their career, please introduce me to them.

If you or someone you know is interested in learning more about the benefits of franchising, please let me know and I will get them next Franchising Is Right seminar.

If you know any business bankers, attorneys or CPA's, please connect me, as I can network through those professionals.

Additional Thoughts On 30-Second Commercials

In constructing your commercial, remember that one commercial does not fit all people, places, or situations. So, you should not limit yourself to just one. Rather work up a series of different 30-second commercials. Here are some thoughts to consider...

Various Message Bodies ... No doubt you have tons to say. So, say it. Just do not cram it all into one commercial. You should have an arsenal of message bodies, each focused on something different.

Creatively Create Confidence ... There is more than one reason why people should refer (or use) you, so share a different one from time to time (whether it's you, your company or the process you use).

Alter The Request ... Being referred clients is wonderful, but it is NOT the only thing that can help you become successful. So, be sure to ask for different things at various times.

Mix Up The Order ... The above framework is a suggested guide. It is not an ironclad rule of thumb, however. Lead with your strong definite request or perhaps an amusing message body. It does not matter how you slice or dice the framework. The key is conveying the message in about 30 seconds.

Finally, once you have constructed a handful of 30-second commercials, you need to make them part of your professional life (whether at a business function or within your personal time). To do this ...

Write Them: Using something as basic as a small note pad or 3x5 cards, neatly write or type your commercials for future reference.

Review Them: Once you have them written out, keep them handy so that you can practice or review them from time to time (just a few minutes each week is plenty).

Use Them: When someone then asks, "Who are you?", do not hesitate. Have the courage to launch into one of your 30-second commercials (picking the appropriate one for the time and place).

Refine Them: Your 30-second commercials are always a work in process. You should look for ways to update them, make them more clear, or better represent you.

Remember, to become a successful franchise broker, you need a strong network of contacts -- people who *know* you, *like* you and *trust* you. The starting point to this is having an arsenal of effective 30-second commercials that convey a sense to... *Who* you are ... *What* you do ... *Why* they should refer you... and, *How* they can help you.

Chapter 7

Advanced Concepts For The Franchise Broker
Using Hard Science To Hone A Soft Skill

Introduction

Achieving success as a franchise broker is about effective networking. As much of networking involves human interaction, sociology and psychology are continually at play.

These social sciences are being heavily studied and this research can be useful in bolstering your networking prowess. In this program, I will share some of this research and how you can capitalize on it to bolster your networking efforts.

Patterns Of Human Interaction

Networking is helping and being helped by others. Really, everything you do with networking can lend itself to making the next sale. For example, attending events where you do nothing more than socialize is networking, but that can lead to sales. Volunteering in the community is networking, and that can lead to sales. Suffice it to say, any networking is productive. Suffice it to say, all networking is ultimately productive. It is simply human interaction and nothing more.

These human interactions are really just the relationships we have with one another. How we connect. Some connections are passing. Some connections are more lasting. Some connections are seemingly lifelong.

Given this, networking is, more or less, really just human behavior. Talking. Listening. Understanding. Being empathetic, encouraging, inspiring, smiling, laughing, and being a friend. Thus, all human behavior involving other people are relationship-based and is networking.

The wonderful thing about human behavior is that there are patterns to it. While the patterns may not be perfectly predictable – as you might find with a chemical reaction or a physics experiment – there are patterns generally there.

Patterns Create Curiosity

Whenever there are patterns, however, there is curiosity. And whenever there is curiosity, you will find people of science trying to explain the patterns through studying, observing, and examining them.

Human behavior involving our relationships is no different. The social sciences – sociology, psychology, and economics, just to name a few – for years have examined how humans relate to one another, both personally and professionally.

Interestingly enough, many of these experiments and studies offer wonderful insight as to how you can both become better at networking as well as have a better network.

While there are likely dozens of these studies (and many more being undertaken at this very moment), the balance of this program is going to examine five in particular.

Network Pyramid Capstones

The first concept we will explore relates to Network Pyramid Capstones. In the 1960's, Harvard social psychologist, Stanley Milgram studied what he termed the "small world" problem. He wanted to gain a better understanding of how people were connected to one another.

In one experiment, he sent to 160 randomly selected individuals in Omaha, Nebraska a packet with the name and address of a stockbroker who worked in Boston (and lived in Sharon, Massachusetts). Milgram instructed each individual to write their name on the roster in the packet and then mail the packet to a friend or acquaintance who they thought would get it closer to the stockbroker, and so on until it reached the Boston broker.

On average the packets reached the broker in six steps (thus the phrase "six degrees of separation"). While Milgram initially reasoned that if the packets started from 160 random points, the packets would arrive at its destination with similar randomness. Many of the chain packets, however, followed the same asymmetrical pattern to the Boston stockbroker.

In all, half of the responses that got to the stockbroker were delivered by three people. Hence, the phrase "six degrees of separation" doesn't mean that everyone is linked to everyone else in just six steps. It does mean that a very small number of people are linked to everyone else in a few steps, and the rest of us are linked to the world through those few.

Lesson: Reconnect With Productive Contacts

There is an easy way to explore this idea. Write down the names of 40 friends and trace them backwards to how they were introduced to you. This exercise will reveal that what people term as their "social circles" are really inverted pyramids, i.e., a large percentage of our contacts originated from a relatively few number of individuals. Those at the tops of these pyramids we refer to as our Network Pyramid Capstones.

Here is the consideration for you as you look to build a franchise brokerage business. If you are working to "jump start" your network or determine where your time is best spent, first, find your Network Pyramid Capstones. Then take one or all of your Network Pyramid Capstones to lunch, breakfast, for coffee or beer or whatever.

That is really make an effort to develop a great relationship with these people – find ways to help them and be sure they understand how they can help you. These individuals have been instrumental in building your network to this point. It is likely they will do more of the same in the future.

Six Degrees Of Kevin Bacon

In addition to the people you should devote networking energy to, you should also have some consideration as to the types of people with whom you network, what we can term "Six Degrees of Kevin Bacon."

To explain this, start with an understanding of the Kevin Bacon game. Kevin Bacon is a relatively well known and popular American actor. The idea behind the game - which is a popular pop culture trivia game - is to link any actor or actress through the movies they've been in, to Kevin Bacon.

Example: Mary Pickford was in "Screen Snapshots" with Clark Gable, who was in "Combat America" with Tony Romano who, 35 years later, was in "Starting Over" with Kevin Bacon. Three Steps.

In the 1990's, computer scientist Brett Tjaden (University of Virginia) using the Internet Movie Database determined that Kevin Bacon was on average 2.8312 steps from any actor or actress (which placed him 668th of all actors and actress). Then using the database, he determined the overall connectivity of every actor and actress in the database. Among the top 50 were names such as Martin Sheen, Robert Mitchum, Gene Hackman, Donald Sutherland, Rod Steiger, and Shelly Winters.

Lesson: Live In Lots Of Worlds

In the magazine *Nature*, Duncan Watts and Steven Strogatz further reviewed this analysis and attempted to determine why an actor such as Burgess Meredith, appearing in 114 films, ranked in the top 20 when Gary Cooper with a similar number of films ranked even behind Kevin Bacon at 878th and John Wayne with 183 films only ranked 160th.

What they concluded was that while Gary Cooper and John Wayne appeared in a significantly greater number of movies, the movies they did appear in where similar movie types. In fact, over 50% of John Wayne's movies were westerns.

Burgess Meredith, on the other hand (who only appeared in approximately 60% of the movies as Gary Cooper and John Wayne) appeared in a wide variety of movies types: 42 dramas (including Of Mice and Men (1939) and Rocky (1976)); 22 comedies; 8 adventures; 7 action; 5 documentaries; science fiction, horror and a western; 4 thrillers; 4 crime movies; 2 children; 2 romance; 2 mysteries; 1 musical; and 1 animated film.

Here is the "take away" from the Kevin Bacon game and the analysis of the relativity connectivity of actors and actresses. First, take a look at your network. If it is unproductive or stagnant, look at whom you are involved with.

Does your network look like Burgess Meredith's career? Great! Does your network resemble the career of John Wayne? If so, work to diversify your network.

If everything you do revolves around work, family, or one group of people, your network will have limited potential. To explore the real potential of your network, however, you need to live in lots of worlds. Get involved at work. Get involved at church, PTA, youth sports. Belong to a trade association outside your profession.

Strength Of Weak Ties

In addition to the types of people with whom you network, to benefit your network you also need to consider your prior relationship with those whom you network. This is known as "The Strength of Weak Ties."

In his 1974 book *Getting A Job*, author and sociologist Mark Granovetter found that 56% of people found jobs through personal contacts. This is not surprising. After all, it is not what you know, but who you know. Remember?

The surprise in his research, however, was that the personal contacts used to obtain these jobs were not from family or close friends. Rather a significant majority of people who found jobs via personal contacts did so via their "weak ties". In fact, 55.6% of individuals reported that they saw their "job-producing" contact only occasionally and 27.8% saw their contact only rarely.

Lesson: Reach Out To Weak Connections

Therefore, when it comes to finding out about new jobs – or, for that matter, gaining new information or looking for new ideas or *finding franchise contacts* – weak ties tend to be more important than strong ties.

Why? Because your close ties tend to occupy the same world as you do. For example, a spouse or close friend might substantially share the same network as you. Thus, they could only refer or connect you to people you already know.

Mere acquaintances, on the other hand, are much more likely to know something or someone that you do not. While you might share a small overlap in networks, most of the people they know are completely unexplored territory for you.

Bringing the concept of The Strength of Weak Ties into your franchise brokerage means this: Do NOT rely on those that you know real well to build your clientele.

Rather, a better means for fortifying your network is to make a point of occasionally associating with people you know, but not that well. The person from work that you sort of knew from occasional meetings or trips up on the elevator. The person at church that you see every week and can address by name, but you know little else about them.

Thus, from a networking perspective, the most important people in your life are the people who aren't closest to you. In fact, the more people you know who aren't close to you, the stronger your position becomes.

In summary, what matters in getting ahead is the quality of your relationship, but one measure of quality is to what extent someone is not particularly close to you.

Having lunch with your long-time best buddy can be fun. It, however, does little to build your network. If you want to build your network, have lunch with someone you know, but not that well (e.g., the friendly stranger).

The Power Of Flocking

We have explored finding your most important networking contacts, understanding how diversity can maximize your networking reach, and how acquaintances have a greater impact than close friends. Now let's turn the attention to how your activities can enhance the value you have to offer.

The United Kingdom has had a longstanding milk distribution system in which milkmen in small trucks bring the milk in bottles to the door of each country house. At the beginning of the 20th century, these milk bottles had no top. As a result, birds had easy access to the cream that rose to the top of the milk in each of the bottles.

In fact, two different species of British garden birds, the titmice and the red robins, most capitalized on this opportunity. Each species learned to siphon off cream from the bottles, tapping this new, rich food source.

In addition to not being sanitary, these birds were stripping the milk of its vital nutritional value. This prompted dairies in the 1940's to start installing aluminum seals on milk bottles. Thus, when the milkman delivered the product, the birds were effectively prevented from getting at the cream.

This only worked for a short while, though. One by one, titmice learned to pierce this weak defense. Before long, the entire titmouse population were only mildly inconvenienced by the aluminum caps.

The same was not true of the robins. As a species, they never learned how to get around the bottle cap and pierce the cream at the top of the milk. Certainly, here and there, one robin would be fortunate enough to figure it out, but as a whole, the species was foiled (no pun intended) from getting at the milky cream, as they once had.

Why was this the case? After all, the robin and the titmouse were very similar birds in size and physical characteristics. The difference was in how the birds interacted within their own species.

The robin is an individualistic bird. They are self-serving and territorial. Rather than cooperate with one another, when one comes near the territory of another, the resident robin will chase off the first.

The titmouse on the other hand is a communal bird, relying on one another heavily for survival. They stick together in tight groups of at least eight to ten. As such, they are able to cooperate and collaborate together, quickly learning what works and what doesn't for one another. They have an efficient social propagation process in which they are able to adapt to changing conditions and learn from each other because of their mutual dependencies.

In short, the titmice almost universally prevailed against the aluminum caps because they learned from one another. After all, that is their way.

On the other hand, while an occasional robin might have gained access to the cream, the successful birds never shared the information with others.

Lesson: Flock Often To Learn

So, what's the lesson for the aspiring franchise broker? Simple: Birds, like the titmice, that flock, seem to learn faster, evolve more quickly, and increase their chances to survive.

This is true for you as well. When you interact with others, you learn. You learn new information. You learn new techniques. You learn how to dress and talk. You probably learned how to open a carton of milk.

In your life, in order to quickly get over obstacles and move past barriers and on to your goals -- such as finding people interested in buying franchises -- you should take every opportunity to behave as the titmouse and help each other succeed together. This would include sharing tips and tricks with one-another or taking an interest in the needs of your peers.

Generosity Stimulus

Flocking with other professionals is just one networking activity that social science has proved to be successful. Another began as a well-known fable. In Marcia Brown's old tale, entitled *Stone Soup*, plague-ridden villagers were stingy with their food and had no interest in sharing with anyone but their own.

This begins to change, however, when a peddler tells the villagers that he would like to share some stone soup with them (essentially throwing a few rocks in boiling water). This action, along with some goading words, moved villagers to become generous -- one by one sharing. A head of cabbage here, some salt beef there, and voila, before long there is a large brew collectively made and fit to feed all of them.

Brown essentially suggests that generosity and altruism are contagious. Is this just a hopeful fable? Or is there any truth to this assertion?

A study that supports this claim was conducted by Nicholas A. Christakis, M.D., Ph.D. and James H. Fowler, Ph.D. They assembled a set of 120 students were put into groups of four. The groups' individuals were given some money to be used to perform an exercise composed of a series of tasks.

Participants both profited and lost via these tasks in a capitalistic exercise. After each exercise, however, the individuals had the option of giving some funds to others at the expense of their own.

After each exercise, the groups were mixed up so that no two groups were ever the same throughout the experiment. In the first few rounds of exercises, no money was gifted to other groups.

Amongst the participants, however, was a confederate -- someone in on the experiment. This person we will refer to as the "Stone

Soup Peddler." After certain exercises, the Stone Soup Peddler started to systematically give away some of the money to others.

In the exercises that followed this exhibition of generosity, the people who benefitted from the gift, gave more. In addition, even the people who witnessed the gifting, but did not directly benefit began giving more. These altruistic gestures then began to spread through the group.

Lesson: You Can Stimulate Generosity

As a franchise broker, you are dependent upon others giving to you. You look for others to give you information. You look for people to share referrals with you. You need people to share insights and ideas with you.

Acts of generosity, however, are inspired somehow. That is people do not just give. Rather people are moved to give somehow, some way. As the story of *Stone Soup* or the Christakis-Fowler study illustrates, you have the power to inspire generosity through your own generosity.

The substance of the act does not matter. What does matter, however, is that you act, as this simple gesture becomes contagious. You can literally inspire your entire network with one small act to literally anyone. A simple referral. An introduction. Sharing of insight or information.

Any or all of this will inspire your network to give to others. In so doing, not only will you have done something wonderful, but you will also be in close proximity when the generous begins to materialize.

Relationships Are Just Human Interaction

Again, networking is helping and being helped by others. It is simply human interaction and nothing more. These human interactions are really just the relationships we have with one another. Some connections are passing. Some connections are more lasting. Some connections are seemingly lifelong.

Given this, networking is, more or less, really just human behavior. Talking. Listening. Understanding. Being empathetic, encouraging, inspiring, smiling, laughing, and being a friend. Thus, all human behavior involving other people are relationship-based and is networking.

The wonderful thing about human behavior is that there are patterns to it. While the patterns may not be perfectly predict-able – as you might find with a chemical reaction or a physics experiment – there are patterns generally there.

Studies Offer Insight

Interestingly enough, many of these experiments and studies of-fer wonderful insight as to how you can become both better at networking as well as have a better network.

While there are likely dozens of these studies (and many more being undertaken at this very moment), this chapter focused on about five science-proven means for improving your networking and your underlying network, including:

1. Reconnect with those in your network who have proven to be productive for you;

2. Have a diverse existence personally and professionally, interacting with lots of different people;

3. Remember that the strongest connections you have are those that you likely know the least (i.e., your weak ties);

4. Be sure to take the time to interact with people (especially

others in the franchise community often), as that is where you stand to get the most; and,

5. Find opportunities to help those around you, because when you do, you increase the likelihood that you get the help you need.

AmSpirit

BUSINESS *CONNECTIONS*

An Opportunity With Great Synergies

The **AmSpirit Business Connections** franchise opportunity offers a great return on investment, but it is also designed to both dovetail with and enhance the franchisee's other business endeavors, because:

- It Only Requires A Part-Time Effort; and,

- The Client Base Is Highly Professional; and,

- The Opportunity Enhances The Franchisee's Professional Network.

If you have a client that is interested in learning more about how **AmSpirit Business Connections** franchise opportunity would enhance his or her other business interest, contact Frank Agin at frankagin@amspirit.com.

Chapter 8

The Franchise Broker Securing Clients
Creating A Referral Machine

Introduction

Achieving success as a franchise broker is about building a network where the broker's network refers them candidates. This chapter offers a practical game plan that any franchise broker can use to make it more likely the broker's network will consistently refer them candidates.

A Three-Step Process

You are ambitious. You want to be more successful. You are savvy. You know that referrals are the most effective means of creating this greater success. The best place to be in business, any business (especially as a franchise broker) is the point where your new clients are almost exclusively generated from people in your network.

These are friends, colleagues, strategic partners and even former clients are sending you prospective clients. At this point, you have effectively created a referral machine. Just because you want this referral machine does not mean that you get it however. There is a process to it, a three-step process.

You start by *establishing relationships*. Then within those relationships (which is essentially a network of people), you *empower them* to not just understand what you do, but how to talk about it. Then finally, you remain in *continual contact* to appropriately guide and re-adjust the process. Yes, this takes work, but in the end the rewards far outpace the effort. The balance of this chapter will review each of these steps in greater detail.

Step 1: Establish Relationships

The foundation upon which you will create a referral machine is based upon the relationships you have with others. This is probably the most important point of this program. Again, *people do business and refer business to those that they know, like and trust.* Those who get the most and best referrals are simply those who have the best relationships, as they are widely *known,* highly *liked,* and implicitly *trusted.*

This all begs two important questions: (1) *With whom* should I establish these relationships? And then even more importantly, (2) *How* do I go about establishing these relationships?

Establish Relationship With Whom?

As to *with whom* you should establish relationships, there is no magic or secrets. They are all around you. First, start with the *people you already know.* Why? The people you already know, presumably already know, like and trust you.

Far too often, when people embark on creating a referral machine, they become fixated on people they have never met before. Think about it. You know tons of people right now - friends from the community or school, former colleagues, existing or past clients. This represents a treasure trove of raw materials with which to work.

Second, develop a list of *strategic partners.* Ask yourself this, who are the people that do not compete with you, but run in the circles as you would like to be running? What is the profile of a good potential client for you and who might be servicing them?

Third, everyone has potential. *Everyone* knows someone who might be a good potential referral for you (they may or may not realize it). This is not to say that you need to establish a relationship with everyone. What it does say, though, *do not* dismiss anyone. Give everyone attention and respect. Remember, every contact has opportunity.

How To Establish Relationships?

You see, there are lots of potential people *with whom* to establish a relationship. That, however, is seldom people's shortcoming in creating a referral machine. It is the *"how"* that trips people up.

In establishing relationships, there are three main categories of activities you need to consider making part of your personal regimen. (1) Giving or *adding values to others*; (2) Ensuring that you *become involved*; and (3) Making sure that you are *dependable or reliable* in what you say and do. Let's examine each one of these in detail.

1) How To Add Values To Others

When people hear the term "giving to others", they tend to conjure up images of dragging out their wallets. That is not the case at all. There are lots of things you can do in giving or *adding value to others,* such as: Do business with others...Sending them referrals...Providing them with information...Spurring them on...Introducing them to others.

Each of these things adds value to others. The key part of all of this, however, is that when you *add value* to others, they cannot help but feel they *know you, like you, trust you.* And somehow, they are quietly compelled to return the deed at some point in time.

2) How To Get Involved?

Another means of establishing relationships, is getting involved within your community.

Trust this, no matter where you live, there are business groups, charities and civic initiatives that could use your time, talent and energy. When you get involved in your community, it raises your level of exposure and it demonstrates your commitment. With these things, people cannot help but feel they know you, like you and trust you, which is exactly what you need to start establishing relationships and create a referral machine.

3) How To Be Reliable

Adding value and getting involved are great for establishing relationships. You, however, will undermine the entire process, if you are not reliable. With even an innocent infraction of unreliability, you can kill your chances getting referrals. Be reliable. Be on time. Do what you say. Follow-up, as you promise. And if for some reason you are unable to do these things, alert the person who might be relying as soon as possible.

This may all seem like common sense. It is. It is, however not common practice. It has tripped up even those with the best of intentions. Guard against this.

Step 2: Empower The Network

Establishing relationships is an important first step. In so doing, you have built a network of people who are really behind you. Again, they know, like and trust you.

This alone does not create a referral machine, however. Before your network can refer you, they need to be empowered. Empowered to *recognize opportunities* for you as well as empowered to talk or *communicate* about you.a

"Opportunity Recognition" Education

People within your network do not magically know how to refer you. First, they need to know **who** to refer you to and they need to know **when** to refer you. To make this happen, it is entirely up to you to empower them to **recognize** these opportunities.

Consider franchise brokerage. Certainly if someone comes out and says, "I am looking to buy a franchise", your network should know to think of and refer you. But what about all the times that someone could be a great client but does not say they are looking to buy a franchise (or they do not even know that franchise ownership is an option).

What about the person whose spouse is looking to have their own business?

What about the displaced executive who might not be interested in getting back into the grind?

What about the mid-level manager that wants a way out of the grind?

If you want to create a referral machine, it is your job to *paint a picture in the minds of your network* as to who is a good referral candidate and what is a good situation. Here are three great ways to do this.

ONE: Develop a series of short elevator speeches that concisely convey what you are looking for and what you do. Again, develop a series, so that you have a varied message. Writing these out and practicing then use them as often as possible. Revisit chapter 6 (Pitching The Franchise Broker... An Effective 30-Second Message.)

TWO: Even if you have a great 30-second commercial, people are not going to fully remember what you have to say. To overcome this, develop (again) a series of short summaries outlining what you are looking for. Make these short and simple (so simple that a 5th grader could understand them) and either have them professional done or neatly type and lay them out with a computer. Then hand and mail (and e-mail) these out consistently.

THREE: If you give people the basic facts, they might politely listen. But if you weave those facts within a compelling story, an example or analogy, they will be enthralled by what you have to say. If you have experiences, share them. If you do not have experiences, then talk to someone who does and borrow theirs. If you have neither experience or access to someone who does, make up examples. In this situation, it is not stealing to make someone else's experiences your own. It is not lying to craft a story that has not occurred. You are doing this to *paint a picture* of what a good referral looks like.

Connection Coaching

If you do a spectacular job educating your network on recognizing referrals, great. That, however, is not enough. You need to empower them with the ability to talk to prospective clients about what it is you do.

For example, if they recognize that the displaced executive is a potential client to refer to you, great. Encourage them to strike up a conversation with the person (and they will if they know, like and trust you). And transition into a discussion about franchising. Here is an example:

"I am sorry you are in transition. What is your next move? Have you considered becoming your own boss? I understand that franchising is almost a fool-proof means of successfully being in business. I know a great franchise broker ... there is no obligation to meet with him and his services are essentially free, as the

franchisors pay his fees."

In addition to general conversation, empower your referral machine with non-technical buzz words and catch phrases about your industry (as well as what they mean) ... Franchise Fee ... Ongoing Royalties ... FDD ... Earnings Claim ... Discovery Day. Your network should know enough to talk about what you do but not enough to do it.

Finally, encourage your network to hook you into the situation. In short, encourage the person to talk about you in a connecting sense. Returning to the example from before *"I know a great franchise broker. There is no obligation to meet with him and his services are essentially free, as the franchisors pay his fees."*

Step 3: Constant Communication

You have established relationships and you have empowered that network. Great! Know this, however, there is no such thing as perpetual motion. Far too often, people work hard to create a referral machine only to watch it "peter out" or break altogether because they erroneously assume that an empowered network will just keep kicking out referrals.

Think of creating a referral machine like pushing a car: You have to work really hard to get the car rolling. Once the car is rolling you do not have to exert much force to keep it moving, but it still takes mild effort (and you dare not let it come to a stop, because then it is like starting over).

With creating a referral machine, the *establishing relationships* and *empowering the network* is the Herculean push to get things moving, the mild force to keep it all moving involves three things.

1) Ask

Yes, continue to ask for referrals, but also ask for things that your network might not see. From time to time, someone will become frustrated with their network because it is not referring something that seems obvious to them. Remember those who make up your referral machine do not live in your world. They do not always see it the way you do. Do not be afraid to ask.

"Can you introduce me to this person?"

"Could you get me an opportunity to speak at this event?"

"Would you keep your eye open for this?"

Do not be afraid that your network will be annoyed. Remember, if you do it right, they know you, like you, and trust you.

2) Appreciate

Second, no matter what your network does for you, thank them. If they send you a referral or do anything of value, fall all over yourself thanking them. Celebrate your joy with them.

If a referral goes nowhere, fall all over yourself thanking them. Why? First, the glass is always half full. The fact they are thinking of you is an excuse enough to celebrate. **Your referral machine is working!**

Second, appreciation is a wonderful motivator. You dole it out and people want more. And they will do what is necessary to get more. Know this, few people "thank" others. Therefore you will really set yourself apart when you show appreciation towards others.

3) Clarify

Finally, no matter how well you educate and empower, your network is going to get it wrong from time to time. They want to help you, but they are going to send you referrals that are, well, bad.

So what? Don't get frustrated. Remember, the glass is half full. They want to help and they are trying. Take the opportunity to reconnect with them and clarify. One small correction in how they are perceiving what is a good referral for you could spell the difference between continued bad referrals and a great new client.

Recapping The Three Step Process

Remember, the best place to be in business, is where you have **created a referral machine**. This is the point where your new clients are almost exclusively generated from people in your network friends, colleagues, strategic partners and even former clients are sending you prospective clients.

This does not come about overnight and it does not occur like magic. It takes work to **establish relationships** and then **empower the network**. Then it takes effort to maintain **continual communication**. All this, however, pays off if you stick to this three-step process.

AmSpirit™

BUSINESS CONNECTIONS

A Great Development Opportunity

In addition to great return on investments and synergies with existing business interests, the **AmSpirit Business Connections** franchise opportunity serves to benefit its franchisee from a personal and professional development perspective, because:

- It Exposures Them To Insightful Thinking; and,

- It Offers Ongoing Experience With Interpersonal Dealings; and,

- It Projects Them As An Expert In Their Community.

If you have a client that is interested in a wonderful franchise opportunity along with the related personal development, contact Frank Agin at frankagin@amspirit.com to learn more.

Chapter 9

Social Media And
The Franchise Broker
Networking Through LinkedIn

Introduction

In the early days of the Internet, companies built websites and then completely took on the responsibility of supplying all the content. Content was (and still is) necessary in order to keep people visiting the website (which was important for generating advertising revenue).

It, however, was a daunting task to generate fresh, interesting content on a continuous basis. As a result, the economic model of many websites failed. This prompted developers to explore ideas for moving away from this notion and look for a new approach to the Internet.

Eventually, some developers seized upon a unique idea. They created websites where ordinary people created the online content using highly accessible and scalable publishing technologies. These developers looked to people like us (and millions others) to write about what is interesting to us and share things we deem to be important or entertaining.

These types of websites we now generally refer to as social media, and these sites have completely shifted how we discover and read online, as well as share news, information, and other content.

LinkedIn: One Of Many Social Media Applications

There are millions upon millions of business people on LinkedIn and these users represent individuals from every developed corner of the world as well as most every professional category and level of attainment. As such, it is a great way of connecting you and your franchise brokerage with others.

Know, however, that while this chapter is geared towards LinkedIn, there is also Facebook and Twitter. Furthermore, beyond these big three, there are dozens of different types of social media. Each of these can connect you to others.

LinkedIn ... A Networking Tool, Not A Replacement

That said, understand this, using LinkedIn is NOT a replacement for networking. It is just another tool for networking.

Think of it in these terms, humans networked with each other long before the invention of the telephone. They interacted as best they could to develop sound personal relationships with each other.

When the telephone came along, however, the underlying networking relationship did not change. The telephone was merely a tool at allowed people to connect farther and faster.

Fast forward to today. The basics of human relationships are much the same as they have always been. As with the invention of the telephone, LinkedIn is merely a tool that allows us to connect farther and faster. LinkedIn, however, does not replace networking. It just makes it easier.

With that notion, do not get so immersed on LinkedIn (or any social media website) that you ignore traditional methods of networking, like attending business functions or picking up the telephone to talk with someone.

LinkedIn: The Networking Event

You have likely been to a local networking event, a gathering of people for getting to know, like, and trust one another. Examples of networking events include gatherings such as business after-hours, Chamber functions or business open houses.

Likewise, LinkedIn is, nothing more than a gathering of people for getting to know, like, and trust others. Given that, LinkedIn is nothing more than a networking event, albeit completely online.

This online networking event known as LinkedIn, however, has three distinct advantages over its traditional counterpart.

Worldwide and Immense: Your average networking event might have a few hundred people all from a local area. LinkedIn, however, boast having over 100 million people participating (with likely 100's of hundreds in your region) and they are scattered all over the world.

Continually Operating: Most networking events operate on a particular day and time. With LinkedIn, you can be part of this networking event anytime as it is going 24 hours a day, 7 days a week, 365 days a year.

Information Rich: When you walk into a networking event and see new faces, you cannot tell who is who or their current status. You just don't know. With LinkedIn, you can find the people you are looking for quickly and you can know a ton about them before you start to interact.

LinkedIn: What Can It Do For Me?

To quickly recap LinkedIn is a powerful tool to help you network and you can analogize it as a giant, ongoing, searchable online networking event. Great! If you are like most, however, the $64,000 question is "What Can It Do For Me?"

First, LinkedIn is an effective means of networking through to people. You can meet attorneys, bankers and those associated with employment transition. In short, LinkedIn is a great way to find and work through strategic partners who can lead you to people seeking to purchase a franchised business, i.e., clients.

LinkedIn, however, is not appropriate for overtly selling your service. Again, remember, it is just like a networking event. As you would not (or should not) consider openly pitching your services at a networking event, it is not advisable to do so on LinkedIn either.

Second, LinkedIn is a wonderful way to position yourself in the hearts and minds of others. If you are like many franchise brokers, you are new to the profession. This means that many of the people who know you, know you as someone else. Even if you have been in franchise brokerage a long time, your online network might not fully appreciate what it means.

LinkedIn provides you a platform to brand yourself as a knowledgeable and committed person in the franchise industry (someone to know, like, and trust). It will not do this overnight, but in time you can establish yourself as a franchising expert on LinkedIn.

Finally, and likely of most interest, LinkedIn is a great means of creating opportunity.

Through it, you can connect with people that can lead you to clients;

Through it, you can find events that can lead you to clients;

Through it, you can get information that can connect you to clients; and,

Through it, clients can become aware of you and connect with you directly.

LinkedIn will not provide a windfall immediately (as some days will be better than others), but over time the opportunity will be there.

LinkedIn: How Can I Make The "What" Happen?

More importantly than the "What Can LinkedIn Do For Me?," is the question of "How Can I Make This WHAT Happen?"

Let's return to the "networking event" analogy. Imagine, you went to a networking event, grabbed a chair, and sat along the wall. What would you expect to gain from the experience? Answer: NOTHING!!!

To make a traditional networking event work for you, you need to do certain things. These would include (but are not be limited to):

Create a presence for yourself in the best possible way;

Congregate amongst people with similar interests; and,

Add value to others by sharing thoughts and information.

LinkedIn is much the same. You can expect nothing from it, unless you put something into it. To realize positive results you need to interact with others. Doing this on LinkedIn falls into four main categories.

1) Creating a Professional Profile;

2) Participating In Groups;

3) Content Contribution; and

4) Share An Update.

We will examine each of these active uses of LinkedIn in detail.

LinkedIn Active Use #1: Creating A Professional Profile

When you head to a traditional networking event, you need to be visible as well as have your best foot forward. The same is true within the online networking event known as LinkedIn. On Linke- dIn, you accomplish this by creating and maintaining a profile for yourself, as this is your face in the crowd at this online networking event.

Note that your LinkedIn profile is essentially your electronic re- sume or brochure. Given that, be sure to take the time to present yourself well. Regarding that, here are some thoughts:

Picture: Add a picture so that people can visualize who you are;

Tagline: Provide a short statement of not just your title (e.g., Franchise Broker), but the value you offer (e.g., "Assisting aspir- ing entrepreneurs find the best franchise to fit their lifestyle and interests.");

Overview: Give a synopsis (similar to a 30-second commercial) of what you are about;

Professional Experience: List your work history (listing any- thing that is reasonably professional in nature);

Education: Provide an overview of your education (as this can serve as means for lending credibility for you as well as be a point of common experience or affiliation with prospective clients or strategic partners);

Recommendations: Request some recommendations on the work you have done for and with others; and,

Achievements: List impressive achievements and other experiences that might not come through in your work history (such as professional designations, awards and recognition).

Use your LinkedIn profile to allow people to know as much as reasonably possible about you. The great thing about this profile is that there is no limit to how often you can revise it. So feel free to keep it up to date or revised it to better reflect who you are.

Also, note that when you do update your profile, your network is subtly alerted (potentially prompting them to come back and view it). This further extents your presence on LinkedIn.

LinkedIn Active Use #2: Participating In Groups

From time to time, people are reluctant to do anything on LinkedIn simply because they feel woefully behind. They rationalize aloud or to themselves, "I have not done anything on LinkedIn and so I am connected to so few people. What is the point of doing anything now?"

Embarking on LinkedIn can seem daunting, especially when you see what others have achieved in terms of connections, activity, and traction. It is easy to have that "I will never catch up" feeling.

Do not despair, however. First, everyone started on LinkedIn with a meager number of connections. So in time, you can and will have an impressive foundation of connections if you stick to it.

Second, there is a quick and easy way for you to become networked on LinkedIn. You accomplish this through the second active use – participating in groups.

Returning to the analogy that LinkedIn is nothing more than a giant networking event, imagine that within this immense, continually running, and information rich event, there are rooms off to the side. Within these rooms are people who all have a common interest or affiliation.

For some, it is the fact that they are all involved in small business or a particular company. For others, it is the fact that they now live in an area or once attended a particular college. And for others it is just a general interest, such as marketing, engineering or accounting.

For the most part, these groups are highly welcoming and continually interested in new members. So find a group or groups that interest you and sign in. And if you cannot find a group that you would like to be part of, LinkedIn allows you to create a group and start to grow it.

There are a couple neat things about groups. First, normally on LinkedIn, you can only invite to connect with those that you already know somehow, some way. So if you are just getting started and only have a few (if any) connections, you might feel as if there is no way (or no one to turn to) to get additional connections.

Once you are admitted to a group, however, your potential connections grows by the size of the group. This is because you are able to invite to connect people who are within the group.

Second, normally LinkedIn only permits you to communicate with the people directly connected to you. Therefore, again, if you have few connections, you have not many people with which to communicate. Once in a group, however, you can directly communicate with all the people within that group.

Consequently, joining or starting groups on LinkedIn and then interacting within those groups is a powerful active use of social

media. For example, if you only have 50 personal, first-level connections, but join a group that has 5,000 members, you have effectively increased your network on LinkedIn 100 fold.

LinkedIn Active Use #3: Content Contribution

Returning to the analogy, think for a moment as to how you might
conduct yourself at a traditional networking event. You add value
to others via your conversations with them.

You start and engage in discussions. You also contribute to discussions that others have started.

You likely answer questions that others have asked. And you also
ask questions that you look for others to answer.

These things add value to the network. More importantly, this still
serves to network you better, as people are most inclined to know,
like and trust those who are adding value. LinkedIn provides these
same interaction opportunities you, which is the third active use –
adding value by contributing content.

If you go into any of the groups you have joined, you will see that
there are usually numerous discussions going on. Jump in. Share
your opinions. Lend some expertise. Reference something you
know.

Beyond joining someone else's conversation, if you feel so compelled, on LinkedIn you can start a discussion of your own. This
can be useful in gathering information and opinions on a topic that
interests you (from people literally all over).

In networking (whether traditional networking or online), adding
value is critical to keeping you on the minds of others. Plus, people
want to associate with those that add value. The third active use of
LinkedIn – contributing content via Group Discussions is an effec-

tive means of networking on this virtual medium.

LinkedIn Active Use #4: Share An Update

Much of the success in traditional networking is from listening. There is also, however, the communicating part as well, which is simply keeping those you know informed about you – the "who, what, where, when and how" of your life.

This does not change on LinkedIn. You need to listen and you need to communicate about yourself. You can accomplish this through the fourth active use of LinkedIn, which is simply taking advantage of the "Share An Update" feature. Through this you can keep those in your LinkedIn network informed as to:

Where you are;

What you are doing; and

What you have to share

Most users of LinkedIn do not make a good use of the "Share An Update" feature. Even those few who use it do not effectively take advantage of this application. Nevertheless, this can be a powerful tool for creating exposure for you and your professional brand.

Found on the home page of your LinkedIn account, you can deploy the "Share An Update" feature in three distinct and useful ways: 1) As a public relations tool; 2) As a vehicle for sharing value to others; and; 3) As a means of engaging other in conversation

"Public Relations" Updates

Imagine having a publicist. That is, someone who tracks your every move and reports it to the world, like you were a political icon, professional athlete, or some Hollywood star. Well with LinkedIn, you can.

Using the "Share An Update" feature you can broadcast on your profile the things you are doing. This can enlighten your LinkedIn network on your activity (personally or professionally), such as who you know, what you are working on and where you are.

By consistently sharing updates on your comings and goings, you allow people to have access to your world. This serves to draw them closer. This also further establishes your brand amongst your LinkedIn network that you are not only involved with franchising but also acknowledge about it.

While you are only limited by your creativity and daily activity, some examples of these types of updates could include:

"Drafting a webinar entitled The Top Seven Reasons To Buy A Franchise."

"Meeting with a client to review part-time and passive ownership franchises."

"Reading the latest issue of Success Magazine. If you are thinking of owning your own franchise, get it and read the article on page 25."

"At the Franchise Broker's Association annual convention learning about the impact that tax law changes have on franchising."

"Attending Discovery Day at Sports Clips."

"Sharing Value" Updates

As mentioned, the key to networking success is adding value to others. This is true whether you are networking in a traditional manner or via LinkedIn. People simply want to associate with those that have something to offer – it is purely human nature.

Using the "Share An Update" feature, you can consistently provide value to your LinkedIn network by offering information, sharing insight or simply making alerts.

While there is a plethora of ideas for sharing value, some examples could include:

> *"Firstar Bank is hosting a trade event geared toward people who want to own their own business."*

> *"For a great article on how to read a Franchise Disclosure document, go t the FranchiseEssentials blog."*
> *"Looking to always have access to your files, check out Dropbox (www.dropbox.com)."*

> *"If you have a 401(k), you can own a franchise business. Do a Google search of Benetrends to see."*

> *"Alert: Capital Brands has waived its training fee to all who franchise before December 31st."*

"Engaging Other" Updates

Networking is about building relationships and relationships are largely built through communication. By its very definition, communication involves both broadcasting and listening to what others broadcast.

Given this, networking on LinkedIn is also about building relationships through communication. Just like contributing content via Group Discussions you can use the "Share An Update" feature to communicate and receive information on LinkedIn.

Note that the amount of content you can post within the "Share An

Update" feature is limited. Nevertheless, you can still effectively attempt to engage your network in conversation through it.

Certainly, there is no guarantee that conversation will ensue, the important point to remember is that by communicating you are more likely to remain on the radar of those in your network. With any luck, however, this activity creates interaction and interaction generally leads to value (which again, draws people to you).

While there are plenty of ways of essentially starting a conversation using this feature, some ideas could include:

"What are the best networking events in town this summer?"

"Drafting a seminar on franchising. What would you like to know?"

"Where can I find local job transition groups in the area?"

"If you are heading to the Chamber after-hours, contact me... here or via e-mail. I would enjoy meeting up there."

"What advice can you give me on exhibiting at the Apex Business Forum?"

LinkedIn: A Reasonable Daily Dose

Again, there are four general active uses of LinkedIn ...

(1) Creating a Professional Profile;
(2) Participating In Groups;
(3) Contributing Content; and
(4) Utilizing Status Updates.

That seems like quite a bit to keep up on and it generally begs the question, "How much time is all of this going to take?" To successfully engage yourself in this immensely-large, continuously running and information rich networking event, you need to devote about 100 hours per year to it.

Now, stated that way, the task seems insurmountable. Here is the reality, however: This translates to only about 20 minutes a day or a couple hours scattered over the course of a week on LinkedIn. That does not seem so bad and you can easily fit it in like this:

In the morning, when you are enjoying a cup of coffee, you might tinker with your profile.

Another day, you take a mid-morning break and interact within one of the groups you've joined.

Then, at some point during the week, while you are waiting for dinner to warm up (or arrive) you jump into a discussion or answer a question.

Finally, when there is a break in the action from the big game you are watching, Share An Update.

It is important to note that there are websites and applications available that will empower you to be more effective interacting and sharing information. While those are beyond the scope of this program, a quick search online and you will find plenty. Whatever the case, you can easily find the time to make an effective use of networking on LinkedIn.

LinkedIn: Measuring the Return On Investment

Another question that often comes up is, "What kind of return can I expect from this activity on LinkedIn?"

First, it is not advisable to put measures on what becomes of time spent at networking events. How could you? Some contacts and connections bear immediate fruit. Others, the productivity might manifest itself weeks, months or years later. There is no worthwhile measure, so why bother.

The same is true of LinkedIn. Do not attempt to measure what comes of your activity. Simply participate consistently and trust that things will come to you. Because in time, it will. What comes from it might not be exactly what you want, and it might not be when and how you want it, but things will come to you.

LinkedIn: Three Important Steps To Success

The key to success on LinkedIn is to follow these three most important steps:

1) *Get Started* (or expand your usage a notch or two);
2) Make time to *take a little action each day*, and:
3) Resolve *to keep after it*.

On LinkedIn, there is a lot to do and much to master and learn. Even the most proficient users of LinkedIn find that they are continually learning new things. But remember, no one is judging you on your proficiency using LinkedIn.

They are only judging you on the value you bring to the network. So, start bringing it today.

AmSpirit
BUSINESS CONNECTIONS

Looking For Mr. Right?

Established small business consulting brand seeking a successful, business growth oriented entrepreneur, sales representative or professional to join in a profitable and supportive franchisor-franchisee relationship. Strong desire to and love of networking, a must. Leadership oriented, a plus. Great sales acumen, good but not necessary. Interested in exploring a journey together? Contact Frank Agin at frankagin@amspirit.com.

Chapter 10

Working Leads For The Franchise Broker
Ensuring The Leads You Buy, Pay Off

Introduction

Part of achieving success as a franchise broker entails working leads purchased. Effectively working leads, however, is simply a matter of effective networking. This chapter will share how to apply the art of networking to the specific franchise broker practice of working leads.

The Key To Success

In franchise brokerage, while from time to time someone will seemingly come out of nowhere, contact you, and buy a franchise, if you relied entirely on that you'd have a frustrating, meager existence.

In most any business, leads (which are also called referrals) are the key to success. Know this, you only have so many hours in a day and you can only have a reasonable presence in a tiny fraction of places that could be productive for you.

If you tap into leads, however, you serve to leverage your efforts. Essentially your lead source becomes a sales force for you. A sales force that works effectively for you 24/7 in and around places you could not reasonably get to. And even places you did not know existed.

Suffice it to say, leads are the key to your success as a franchise broker. After all, you are not selling a $50 item that someone is going to buy on a whim. You are selling opportunity that cost tens of thousands of dollars in cash and a total commitment of time and energy.

Types Of Leads

Leads are important. That is a given. Understand, however, that leads fall into two general categories. 1) Those you purchase from a reputation franchise source; and 2) Those leads you acquire through networking, with strategic partners, friends & family, and other others. This second category would also include leads from your website, social media efforts, as well as newsletters and professional programs.

Now some franchise brokers – new and old – may tell you, "I don't pay for leads." You might adhere to that logic as well. Whether you do or you don't know this: All leads come at a price. Whether you purchase them or network for them, you incur a cost.

Purchased leads cost you cash. Networked leads cost time, effort, and social capital. This is not to say one is better than the other. The point is that every lead you get, you pay for somehow.

Thus, you should not swear off purchased leads as a cost savings measure. If you do, you are fooling yourself. Unless your networked activity has you so occupied with potential clientele, consider purchasing leads to supplement your activity.

Value Maximization

Whether you choose to purchase leads, network for them, or some combination of the two, your objective should be to maximize the value you get from leads. Obviously, right? Every lead you get, you hope results in a client purchasing a franchise.

That is not the reality, however. Yes, some leads result in a sale. No doubt on those you have maximized the value of the lead. This is not about those leads. Rather, this chapter is about maximizing the value of those leads that may not result in a franchise sale.

Contact Lead

Whether the lead is purchased or networked, the typical franchise broker will likely follow the below approach in working the opportunity. Once they have the lead in hand, they will make contact with the person. At this point, one of two things will generally occur.

First, the lead expresses immediate interest: *"Yes, I am ready to explore the notion of buying a franchise."* Now there is no guarantee this will happen. Nevertheless, this is a hot prospect. Great. Prudence and good business sense, dictates that you follow up on this as much and as often as reasonably possible given the circumstances. These situations are likely a small percentage of leads you obtain from any source.

Second, for whatever reason, the lead just does not have immediate interest in pursuing franchising. Not ready. Change of heart. Financing issues. Spouse is not in agreement. The list could go on. Whatever the case, there is no immediate interest in moving forward. These situations are likely an extremely high percentage of leads a franchise broker will obtain from any source. At this point, the typical franchise broker will deem the lead a bust, terming it a waste of time, money and effort.

"No" Is

Here is the problem with that mindset, however. In the business sales world seldom does "NO" mean "NO." This is true in franchising as well.

A "NO" might mean "Not Now" – effectively translated to *"I am not interested here today (or maybe not tomorrow or the next), but there may come a day when I might be."*

Additionally, a "NO" might mean "Not Me" – effectively translated to *" I am not interested and likely never will be, but that does not prevent me from referring on someone, at some point, who would be."*

Given these two alternative meanings to the word "NO," very seldom does a lead become a complete and utter waste of time, money, or effort. At worse, the NO is just a diversion or delay in you realizing a return on the monies, time, or effort you expend.

Altering Your Contact Lead

Given this revelation, you (as the savvy franchise broker you are) should alter your prospective franchise candidate decision tree as follows.

Again, the lead that expresses immediate interest ("Yes, I am ready to explore the notion of buying a franchise") you are all over, just like before.

The change is, however, in that second group - the extremely large percentage of leads whom (for whatever reason) do not have an immediate interest in pursuing franchising. Under this revised approach, rather than deeming the lead a complete waste of time, money, and effort, you default to Plan B.

Plan B: Stay On Their Radar

What is Plan B? It is simply recognizing that for whatever reason these people do not have an immediate interest in pursuing franchising, that their "NO" does not actually mean "NO" but rather "Not Now" or "Not Me."

The trick at this point is to keep yourself on the radar of these people until the "Not Now" becomes "Now" or they feel comfortable referring you to someone else.

This then begs the question: What can I do to stay on someone's radar?

"Stay On The Radar" Game Plan

Staying on a prospect's radar is a process. It involves three intertwined activities, each this chapter will explore in detail:

1) Building a relationship with the prospective client;

2) Using some sort of means for consistently documenting the information you learn as well as ensuring that you have systematic communication with the prospect; and,

3) Offering and sharing value with the prospect so that they are interested in your ongoing communication (plus keeping your ultimate objective subtly relevant).

Build A Relationship

As I said before, all things being equal, people do business with (and associate with) those they know, like, and trust. This is a theme that has run through almost this entire book. An effective means of doing this is to take the time to get to know the people behind the leads you acquire.

Whether you purchase leads or get them through networking, these are not just clients making a "dime store" purchase via you. They are people. They have lives and those lives are filled with stories.

As such, do not start your conversation "getting down to brass tacks." Learn about them. Ask them to tell you about themselves. Who are they? Where do they live and where are they from? Where did they go to school? What got them to this point in life? Really try to understand what makes them tick.

Understand, however, this is not an interview. Rather, it is a conversation. Learn about them and genuinely be interested. But also share relevant details about yourself. In so doing, you demonstrate that you are a person too and you demonstrate that you have things in common with them by sharing your own professional and personal stories.

As you converse, you will gain a sense as to who they truly are. You will, in a roundabout way, get at why they are interested in franchising? And that is something you want to learn.

Understanding this, however, you might not get at everything you want to know or need to know in a single conversation. Again, you are building a relationship and not just trying to execute a transaction. Some people are going to be very revealing and others a little more guarded. That is okay. Take it at their pace.

The point is simple: If you seek to truly become a friend to them, in the end you will likely have a client (whether it is them or someone else). If you only want them as a client, you will likely end up disappointed (and someone else will get the business).

Document Intel

As you build a relationship, you will learn things. Somehow, keep track of it. Do not rely on your memory alone. Document it, so they you can review it and refer back to it.

Sure, remembering details about one or two people is a snap. Keeping that same information for a dozen, then a few dozen, and then ultimately hundreds is a different story. As your database of contacts grows, it will become a challenge to keep all the facts, figures, and impressions straight.

Certainly, you could keep track of all of this on loose-leaf pages in a three-ring binder. In the "computer" age why would you? The marketplace has various inexpensive (and some free) customer relationship management tools that are specifically designed for this. In fact, it is likely whatever contact database you are using (such as Microsoft Outlook) has all the bells and whistles that you need.

Whatever the case, devise or find a system that will help you keep track of information. Additionally, however, the systems should allow you to keep track of when you communicated last as well as remind you when you need to re-connect. It should also help you keep track of not just the subject of prior conversations but also keep track of future topics to discuss.

Offer & Share Value

Again, there are three elements to this process. Each is important. Building a relationship and documenting what you learn are important. It will build your knowledge of the prospect and keep the prospect on the top of your mind.

It is, however, not enough to keep them on your radar. Rather YOU need to be on the radar of your prospects. What does is best of all offering and sharing value.

Think of this analogous situation. Imagine you attend an ongoing series of business afterhours (also known as networking events). At each, there is one particular person whom, whenever you encounter them, they remark, in so many words, *"Look at me. Let me tell you all about me and my business."* The first time, you will allow it. The second you are humored. The third you become annoyed. From that point forward, you avoid the person. Why? There is nothing of value to attract you to the situation.

Consider, however, the same series of events and another person. Whenever you encounter this second person, you get not just delightful conversation, but ideas, insight and information. No doubt, at every event you are seeking that person out. They are continually on your radar. Why? The value they offer keeps them there.

If you want to stay on your prospect's radar, there needs to be value. It is important to note, however, that value you have to offer needs to be more than *"I am servicing you by helping you find a great franchise."* That is a transaction that serves to benefit you as much as them, arguably. The value you offer needs to be something of value to them and them alone. And there needs to be no expectation of anything for you. Certainly, you can hope that something comes from the value you share, but there should be no expectation.

This certainly begs the question: What value do I have to offer? Likely lots if you think about it.

For example, in talking with a prospect they express concern about financing. You can take the time to gather information on tapping into a 401(k) or other financing options and get it to them.

Or perhaps, you learn that they are interested in a retail franchise. You can find an article related to the retail industry that you share.

Or even, if you learn that a prospect has an interest in photography, then when you stumble across an article related to that subject you can share it.

This list is seemingly endless. You continually stumble across things that could help your prospective clients. And it is not just limited to information, but also contacts or other items related to your own personal or professional background.

As for how much value you need to share, there is no hard and fast rule. Not every communication needs to create value, but you should offer enough value so that they tend to think of you as someone who is more about adding value than just making a sale.

Some of you may be wondering, *"What if they already had the information, contact, or value, I shared?"* That is okay. Keep trying. In the short run, it is the thought that counts. While at some point, you need to convey actual value to be branded as someone who is value-oriented, do not refrain from trying simply because they might already have the value. You just never know.

The Plus

To quickly re-cap this chapter thus far, following the "Stay On Their Radar" Game Plan you have...

1) Built a relationship with the prospect;

2) Consistently documented the information you learned as well as ensured that you systematically communicated with the prospect; and,

3) Offered and shared value with them.

If you routinely do these things, it is perfectly acceptable to occasionally

Remind them of what you do ("Remember, I am not just in the know on financing a franchise, but I work to help individuals just like you get into the right franchise.").

Ask them for consideration ("If you are thinking of purchasing a franchise, I would appreciate it if you would work with me.").

Ask for referrals or contacts ("Should you know of someone considering purchasing a franchise, I would appreciate you introducing me to them.").

After all, if you are adding value to them, they will not be offended at all by any of this. Moreover, if they know, like, and trust you, they will welcome an opportunity to help you.

Three Important Considerations

Like anything, there are some additional considerations relating to ongoing communication with prospective clients.

First, be appreciative of anything and everything. Thank them for their time. Thank them for responding to e-mails. Even thank them when they tell you to "stop contacting them," as they have just saved you time. Do not look at showing appreciation as one more thing you need to do. Rather look at it as one more opportunity to communicate with them. Plus, understand that taking the time to say "thank you" is becoming a lost art, as few people do it. Thus, you can certainly set yourself a part by being part of the small minority.

Second, be open-minded. This whole process of building relationships and having ongoing communications is nothing more than networking. As has been stated time and again throughout this book, networking works. It might not work how you want it to work, or when, or where, but it will work. Thus, some prospect might not become a client or refer a client, but might benefit you in some other way that today you cannot comprehend. Whatever the case, networking worked. Embrace that.

Finally, this process is not magic. It will not create overnight results. Patiently persist. Don't measure the results over a few days, a few weeks, or a few months. Work it diligently. Things will come from it. Again, networking works.

"No" In Review

In review, remember, not every lead you get (whether you purchase them, network for them, or some combination of this) will result in immediate interest in purchasing a franchise. Nevertheless, with every lead you get there is value, as "No" does not necessarily mean "No." As a savvy franchise broker, you now know that you need to mine that value by keeping yourself on your prospect's radar.

"Stay On The Radar" Game Plan Review

To stay on their radar, remember, you need to:

1) Build a relationship with the prospective;

2) Consistently document the information you learn as well as ensure that you systematically communicate with the prospect;

3) And (arguably most importantly), offer and share value to keep them interested in having you around.

If you routinely do these things, you will position yourself to re-mind them occasionally about what you do, ask to represent them, and ask for referrals.

AmSpirit
BUSINESS *CONNECTIONS*

Franchise Opportunity

AmSpirit Business Connections is a service-based membership organization for entrepreneurs, sales representatives, and professionals. To become a member, these business types pay fees to belong and participate.

These members then meet each week (with an assigned group of other business types) for approximately one hour and 15 minutes to participate in a proprietary structured meeting format where they learn about one another's business and identify referral opportunities for each other.

Franchisees help these groups of members by helping them become larger and more productive in terms of referrals. Franchisees realize a return on their investment of time and money via the membership fees.

If you have a client that may be interested in a professional franchise opportunity or if you would like to learn more about **AmSpirit Business Connections**, contact Frank Agin at frankagin@amspirit.com

Chapter 11

Passive Selling For The Franchise Broker
Capitalizing On Content Marketing

Introduction

As I have asserted time and again in the book, achieving success as a franchise broker is less about selling and more about developing relationships, which we refer to as "networking." Further, a central theme in networking is that it is about providing value to others.

In short, people are drawn to and associate with those who offer some sort of perceived value. It does not have to be significant or immediate, but there needs to be something holding their focus – potential referrals, contacts, information, other support, something.

So if you are looking to drawn people to you (which is just another word for marketing), you need to have a value or reason. A great way to provide value is to share important content with those you know. This, marketing types, generally referred to as "content marketing."

Broker Realities

As an aspiring franchise broker, there are three realities that you need to embrace:

Reality #1 ... Professional Status: You offer a professional service, no different than an attorney or accountant. You have specialized training as well as a unique knowledge base. Moreover, what you do involves a commitment of time and understanding your client's unique situation. *You are a professional.*

Reality #2 ... Franchise Acumen: People do business with those that they know, like and trust, especially when it comes to professional services. As a professional, your clients (and prospective clients) need to know, like and trust you. They need to have every confidence that you "know your stuff" relative to franchising. People are going to use you (as a franchise broker) because you offer something they cannot (or do not want to) do themselves. *So, you need to somehow communicate to your clients (and prospective clients) that you have a significant acumen when it comes to franchising.*

Reality #3 ... Reserved Approach: At the same time, you CANNOT directly tell them how wonderful you might be. If you do, your clients (and prospective clients) consider your direct overtures about your expertise as mere salesmanship and thus largely tune them out. Think about it: If someone in business tells you how wonderful they are, you chalk it up to them trying to make a sale. *So, while you must communicate a professional acumen, you must be reserved in doing so.*

The Dilemma

These three realities create a dilemma: On the one hand, you need to communicate somehow your expertise to clients and prospective clients. Again, it is about know, like, and (mostly) trust. They need to have these three elements or they will find another solution (whether that is another franchise broker or buy a franchise without one).

If you, however, directly communicate how wonderful you are, what you have to say will be discounted or disqualified as mere marketing ... salesmanship ... professional bravado.

These requirements (you need to communicate competency ... but do not communicate directly) seem to create a dilemma (as, if you don't communicate; you are lost in the crowd). I prefer to look at this dilemma as a challenging obstacle or wall you need to penetrate.

History And Folklore As A Teacher

History and folklore are wonderful teachers, so learn from them. Consider this, the ancient city of Troy built a wall around it, largely to keep out the Greeks. It worked. Year after year, the Greeks tried and they continually failed. The Greeks could not get in.

One day, however, they devised a plan. Rather than continuing to attempt to penetrate, the Greeks pretended to abandon their pursuit. Sailing away, however, they left a large, wooden horse. A gift to the City of Troy, it seemed. Troy claimed victory and accepted the gift, bringing it inside walls.

Unbeknownst to them, however, the Greeks hid 30 great warriors inside. In the middle of the night, these warriors snuck out of the wooden horse, opened the gates to the City of Troy, and let in their Greek compatriots. Together, these warriors and Greek army conquered Troy, with the help of a wooden horse.

Trojan Horse Marketing

In the professional services world (which, again, is the franchise broker world), content marketing is much like a Trojan Horse. In other words, content marketing is a means of allowing you to penetrate the seemingly insurmountable "communication wall" with your clients (and prospective clients) in a very reserved manner.

More explicitly, content marketing will allow you to communicate that which you need to say (positioning or branding you as the "franchising expert"). If, however, you do your content marketing right, it will be done so in a manner that your prospective clients will not realize you are building yourself up.

103

What is Contenting Marketing?

Again, content marketing is sharing (very indiscreetly) valuable information and tidbits that paint you as a "subject matter expert," that in time (if done correctly) will cause clients, and prospective clients (and those who know prospective clients) to think of you when the notion of purchasing a franchise comes up.

Examples of content marketing are all around us. The real estate agent that offers a free "first time home buyer" seminar is practicing content marketing. The financial advisor who sends you periodic newsletters on retirement planning advice is practicing content marketing. The Cancer Treatment Centers of America is practicing content marketing when it pays to have an article published in a magazine entitled "Four Things Every Cancer Patient Must Do."

In each of these examples, the entity practicing content marketing could have simply purchased an advertisement or undertook another means of marketing. For far less money, however, they branded themselves in the minds of many, many more prospective clients through this practice.

Content Marketing Is Legit

To be clear, content marketing is NOT a gimmick. It is NOT a manipulation. It is NOT a bait and switch. It is a completely, 100%, genuine means of building yourself up by adding value to others.

It is a means of utilizing well-settled human nature that says "we tend to trust and want to associate with those who bring us value." Thus, content marketing is truly a gift of your knowledge, know-how, and insight. It is something you share freely with NO EXPECTATION of anything in return (but you can trust that it will pay dividends in time).

There is a saying in advertising: "50% of your advertising dollars are wasted; you don't know what 50%." The gist of this statement is that you need to spend money on advertising. While you should be wise about it, you need to understand that much of what you spend will not yield anything. Alternatively stated, do expect that every time you advertise you will get positive results.

Similar, you should understand that, in time, content marketing will create significant results for you. That said, not every content marketing communication you will make will generate results. In fact, the results you those results will be generated by only a small percentage of those who hear your message. Moreover, you should figure that only 20% (or less) of the people exposed to your content marketing will ever acknowledge the message. You do not know who those people are until after the fact, however. So, share your message with as many people as you can.

How To Conduct Contact Marketing

Let's switch gears from "What Is" content marketing, to "How" can you take advantage of it. First, as a franchise broker, there are dozens and dozens of topics that you can talk to and about.

What should someone look for in a quality franchise broker?

Advice for working with a broker.

What are the various types of franchises? One-by-one. Plus and minuses

What are the steps involved in purchasing a franchise?

Review the aspects of FDD and what to look for?

Questions for Discovery Day?

There really is no end to the topics and ideas for finding good content to share. Take 30 minutes and start brainstorming topics. No doubt, you will be able to come up with dozens of topics.

If you exhaust your own creativity, capitalize on the creativity of others. Start by looking at franchise magazines. You can also get on the Internet and see what others have to say. You can also spend some time on LinkedIn reading what others have to say.

None of this suggests that you should plagiarize someone else's work. Rather, use what they have done to: 1) Spark ideas of your own; or, 2) Put a fresh perspective on their ideas; or, 3) Write something that is merely a quick discussion of their work, and then do them the favor of linking back to their work product.

More or less, through content marketing, you are giving them (in tidbits over time) everything they need to know to buy a franchise. You are effectively giving them enough so that they do not need you.

Rest assured, however, that there is so much information on franchising, many people (and likely most) will realize that they do need you. Remember, in professional services (which franchising brokering is), the best way to sell something, is to give it away for free. How is this?

When you share this content marketing value, people cannot help but trust you. When you share this content marketing, you remain on these individual's radar. When you share this content marketing information, they see you as the expert (and when someone is looking to invest five or six figures into a franchise, they will want to use an expert).

Quick Thoughts on Content Marketing

As you plan to and embark upon your content marketing campaign, here are some things to keep in mind.

First, remember that "less is more." In other words, more often than not, a few short paragraphs is far more powerful than an entire newsletter. Plus, you will be more apt to keep up with meaningful content.

Second, you do not need to limit your content marketing to franchise related material. You can really work into your content anything related to business, as that all has relevance to franchising and it goes to demonstrate your broad-base of knowledge.

Finally, while it is tempting to self-promote yourself, resist the temptation. Remember the Third Reality from above: "*People tend to ignore or discount self promotion.*" If you must, however, limit yourself to less than 10% of your communications.

Getting Content Out

There are as many types and means of distributing the content you have, as you have topics to communicate about.

There are in-person programs, such as seminars, workshops, and speaking engagements. Your content marketing could be written, as such articles or newsletters (whether online or a hard copy edition). You could make your content marketing visual (through video, powerpoint, or via PDF graphics) or audio (such as podcasts and Internet radio).

When it comes to content marketing, you can do so by any means you are comfortable in getting what you know in the hands of others.

Key Ingredients

It is important to note that there is nothing about content marketing that implies a major investment. Yes, it requires a little time and yes, it might cost some money (for letterhead, graphics and similar items). There are three key ingredients that you must infuse into your content marketing campaign.

Consistency: You must undertake communication on a reasonably reliable consistent basis. Content marketing is a marathon and not a sprint. Thus, you must commit to something that you can undertake comfortably for a couple (not days, weeks or months) years.

Resilience: Once you start a content marketing campaign, keep going. If you start and stop, you lose all your momentum (which will make it harder to get going again). You need to make content marketing a habit. Just like buying leads. Just like going to networking groups or events.

Patience: I am going to tell you that nothing is likely going to happen immediately. Maybe something will, but it is not likely. Remember, however, the scope of your content marketing campaign is not measured in days, weeks, or months ... but years. Remember this: *You will never be closer to success than when you feel like quitting the most.* Remember, you are planting trees, and not picking fruit. It is going to take time.

Chapter 12

The End Of The Beginning
Time To Get Started

Whew! There is much in this little book. I hope it gets the little gears in your head turning. I want for it to getting you thinking about what you have been doing (or perhaps what you have not been doing) and how you can improve on it. In addition, I intend for it to fill your head with ideas and notions of what you can be doing.

I don't want this book to be an inspiration, however. Inspiration is fun. It's exciting. It can be euphoric. It tends to fade, though ... and usually fast.

I want this book to give you a healthy dose of optimism. If you are honest (at least with yourself), you can probably admit that a time or two since you started in as a franchise broker, you have contemplated quitting (or at least scaling back) and moving on to something else.

No doubt, there is a certain allure to helping someone find the right franchise, seeing them invest upwards of six figures into it, and knowing that 40-percent of it is your. That is probably what drew you to franchise brokering. You now know that finding and closing on those situations falls under the head of "easier said than done." In short, you have to work for it.

With this book in hand, however, I trust you have a degree of optimism that you are now better able to make these situation happen (not overnight, but certainly in time). In short, you now have a greater control over your destiny

Mostly, I want this book to motivate you into action.

Know this, if after reading this book you find yourself with idle time, know that it is the product of a networking deficiency. In short, you have not done the things you need to do from a relationship-building standpoint to create for yourself a steady pipeline of clients

Do not despair, however. It is never too late to get started (or restarted) or just do something. Take a few moments to review this book and then set yourself in motion.

Of course, I am always happy to help. If you have questions related to professional networking, contact me at frankagin@amspirit.com.

About The Author
Frank J. Agin

Frank Agin is the founder and president of **AmSpirit Business Connections**, an organization that empowers entrepreneurs, sales representatives and professionals to become more successful through networking.

As **AmSpirit Business Connections** has grown, Frank has established himself as an authority on professional networking and business relationship development. He has written various articles on professional networking, is a sought after presenter on this topic (including using social media in business) and consults with companies and organizations on how to make a more effective use of business relationships.

Finally, Frank's the author and co-author of several books, listed on the pages that follow or at http://www.frankagin.com/

Along with having a CPA designation, he has an undergraduate economics and management degree from Beloit College (Beloit, Wisconsin) and an MBA and law degree from the Ohio State University. Contact him via e-mail (frankagin@amspirit.com)

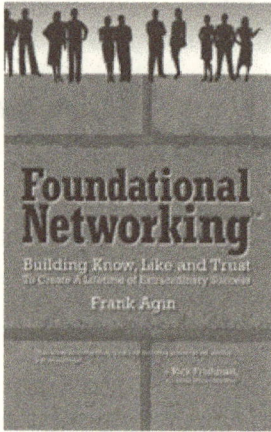

Foundational Networking:
Building Know, Like and Trust To Create A Lifetime of Extraordinary Success

"Become the person you want to network with"

Foundational Networking is a personal development book aimed at helping become better networkers by simply having better attitudes and habits. Released October 2008.

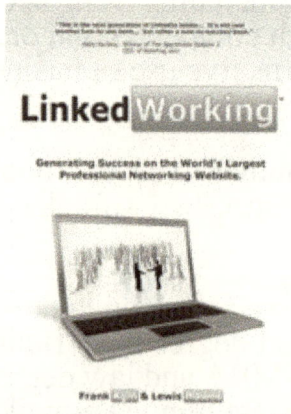

LinkedWorking:
Generating Success on the World's Largest Professional Networking Website

"Success on LinkedIn follows all the same rules of traditional networking."

LinkedWorking is a professional development book aimed at helping individuals achieve great success on LinkedIn, the world's largest professional networking website. Released March 2009.

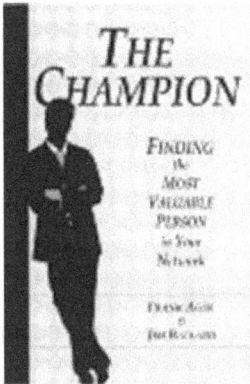

The Champion:
Finding the Most Valuable
Person in Your Network

"Who Is The Most Valuable Person In Your Network?"

Are you looking for a Champion? Don't you sometimes wonder: "There must be someone out there who will set me up with all sorts of great ideas, wonderful opportunities, and incredible new contacts, so as to bring me the success I deserve." If this is your dream *The Champion* will help you find such an individual. Released March 2010.

The Giving Journal:
Achieving Success Through
Focused Generosity

"How Can You Give More To Others?"

The Giving Journal is for anyone who wants more business referrals and clients, more quality contacts and valuable information, more out of a long, happy life, and knows that a focus on generosity can help them achieve it. Released September 2012.

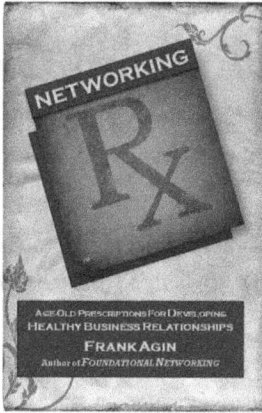

Networking Rx:
Age Old Prescriptions for
Developing Healthy Business
Relationships

*"You have done nothing along.
Everything you are and everything
you will be is a function of the aid,
support, and assistanceof those
around you. In short, it is all the result
of networking and that has been around forever."*

Networking Rx contains dozens of time honored ideas and insights
that you can use today to generate networking success. Released
2013.

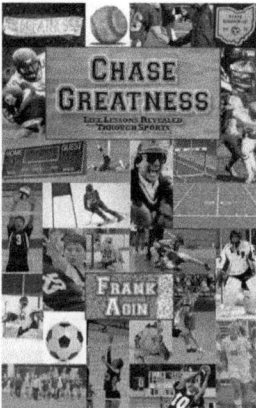

Chase Greatness:
Life Lessons Revealed
Through Sports

*"Sports give you a front row seat
to moments of great humanity.""*

Chase Greatness uses dozens of sports stories that can be used as
teachable moments to help you look for motivation, search for inspiration and chase greatness. Released 2014.